MATTHEW W. CERTO

FORMULAIC

HOW THRIVING COMPANIES
MARKET FROM THE CORE

FORMULAIC

How Thriving Companies
Market from the Core

Matthew W. Certo

ISBN: 0692805842
ISBN 13: 9780692805848

For Farrah, whose kindness and encouragement mean the world to me.

Philippians 4:8

ABOUT THE AUTHOR

Matt Certo serves as CEO and principal of Findsome & Winmore, an Orlando, Florida–based digital marketing agency. He is also the author of *Found: Connecting with Customers in the Digital Age.* Originally called WebSolvers, the company's first client was his alma mater, Rollins College. Matt built the college's first website out of his dorm room at the age of nineteen.

Since then, Matt has grown the company into a fully integrated digital marketing agency by recruiting the region's top marketing and technology talent, adding leading brands to the firm's client roster, and integrating traditional services like brand marketing and public relations. Apart from the growth of the company, Certo's work in the industry has been extensive. He coauthored a book in 2001 (*Digital Dimensioning: Finding the ebusiness in Your Business*) and was asked by the White House to speak at a domestic economic forum with President George W. Bush. In 2016, he visited the White House and spoke regarding President Barack Obama's Computer Science for All initiative.

He is a frequent guest speaker on topics including marketing, web strategy, and search engine optimization, an area in which he has also testified as an expert witness. His clients have included the likes of National Retail Properties, Darden Restaurants, Newman's Own Organics, Foundry Commercial, and Waste Pro. He is a frequent guest speaker to various marketing, advertising, and public relations trade associations and has been widely quoted in publications including *Inc.* magazine, *Business Insider*, the *Huffington Post*, the *San Diego Union Tribune*, the *Boston Globe*, and the *Orlando Sentinel*.

An active community participant, Matt has served as board chairman of a number of nonprofit organizations, including Ronald McDonald House Charities of Central Florida and the First Tee of Central Florida, an organization that he founded. He has also served for more than a decade on the board of the Edyth Bush Charitable Foundation and as chairman of its endowment committee. Certo also serves on the Florida board of managers for Nemours Children's Hospital. He has been recognized by the *Orlando Business Journal* as one of its "Most Influential Men to Watch" and made its "40 Under 40" list three times.

ADVANCE PRAISE FOR FORMULAIC

I found *Formulaic* to be a thought-provoking read for any sized business. Many so-called "marketing" books focus on one element of marketing, and while brand and promotion are important elements of any marketing plan, thinking through your entire offering is essential to success. *Formulaic* provides this framework in a simple and insightful manner.

Brian E. Miller
Executive Vice President
Sales, Marketing and Service Operations
Marriott Vacations Worldwide

Through Matt's years of experience hearing companies and clients cry for "HELP!" he brings us back to the foundational questions of why, what, and how we do things in our businesses. *Formulaic* is a great book that helps us look internally first, before we frame our external message.

Karl Droppers
President
MVP Sports Clubs

In *Formulaic*, Matt does a great job demystifying the magic bullet by dispelling the magic itself and illustrating the importance of not only the bullet, but also the gun and the shooter, in building an enduring and thriving brand. I thoroughly enjoyed his approach in breaking down an otherwise complex issue into smaller, more understandable elements, the importance of which few appreciate.

John Rivers
Founder & CEO
4 Rivers Smokehouse

In this new world order, small, fast, and smart companies can beat the Goliaths of the world on many fronts. Having a solid marketing foundation (and a great product) is the only way to compete. *Formulaic* is a great resource to help owners and companies navigate the marketing world by focusing first on what's important.

Paul Ellis
CEO
Foundry Commercial

Formulaic gets to the bottom of what makes a brand truly great: working from the inside out. Certo's insights and recommendations are relevant whether you're a new business, a long-time social service provider, or something in between. Whatever your enterprise, *Formulaic* makes identifying your unique value and bringing it to the marketplace both understandable and manageable.

Michael Shaver
CEO
Children's Home Society of Florida

ACKNOWLEDGMENTS

The journey of writing a book is one filled with ups and downs. Getting it to a finished product takes a ton of time, patience, and a whole lot of teamwork. I'm grateful to those around me who have been a part of that team.

For starters, the team at Findsome & Winmore has been incredibly supportive. Fellow agency leaders Kelly Lafferman, Rich Wahl, and Kelly Rogers have been both encouraging and instructive. Creative director Andy MacMillin and production specialist Jordan Damato have helped to make the cover art and interior treatments fit the message. Jaylen Christie and Aliyah Shariff have been instrumental in helping to plan and implement this book's promotion. My assistant, Mary Jarrell, has helped me get through each step and create the space in my calendar to develop this material.

My clients inspire me every day and give me a framework to bring new ideas to them from the field and to share in the education and experience of it all. Together, we have learned to thrive. Individuals like Paul Ellis and Nick McKinney (Foundry Commercial), Brial Miller (Marriott Vacations Worldwide), Karl Droppers (MVP Sports) and Mike Shaver (Children's Home Society of Florida), have helped me by both trusting and challenging me in my journey to create this work.

My family members are infinitely important to me—more than they know. My father, Sam, and mother, Mimi, have always provided me with more support and encouragement than I deserve. My siblings Trevis, Sarah, and Brian, along with their families, have all served as supporters and sounding boards in their own special ways. To all of them, I am profoundly grateful.

And to three very special people in my life—Farrah, Porter, and Drew—thank you for always cheering me on and for telling me that *Formulaic* is your favorite book before you had even read it!

TABLE OF CONTENTS

PREFACE

Growing up, I lived across the street from a car broker. Mr. King was a nice man, and he used to visit the auto auction every Tuesday, usually returning with a handful of cars that would sit in his driveway or on his car lot until he sold them. He had everything: pickup trucks with big tires, sports cars with loud engines, and big vans that could double as campers. I'd watch them rotate through the driveway through my bedroom window and was always fascinated.

One day, he showed me a new sports car he had bought and was preparing to sell. I'm pretty sure it was the coolest thing my nine-year-old eyes had ever seen. It was compact, low to the ground, and featured a red racing stripe along the entire length of the bright white paint finish. The panels of the sunroof could even be removed by hand and stored within the hood. I was in awe of the form, shape, and visual appeal of this incredible machine. I decided then and there exactly what I would do when I was old enough to drive. "Mr. King, I'm going to start saving now for this car. This is exactly what I want to drive when I turn sixteen. Will you help me find one when I'm ready?"

Mr. King, who had the appearance and demeanor of Santa Claus, chuckled and commenced to give me one of my first lessons in marketing. "I don't think you want to do that," he said. "These cars aren't very good. They don't ride particularly well, and they break down a lot. And when they do, it's hard to find parts for them because they're uncommon. Mechanics in Indiana aren't familiar with these cars, and it's hard to find someone to repair them. Plus, there's no back seat or trunk, which makes them pretty unpopular with most people. In fact, I doubt this car will continue to be made beyond next year. They're not selling well. All sizzle and no steak."

I was disappointed for sure, because my dream car seemed to appear and vanish within a few brief moments. But the story has stuck with me for decades because of the truth that Mr. King revealed to me without knowing it: appearances and veneer are alluring, but they alone can't fix a bad product or prevent a seasoned buyer from seeing through a sleek exterior all the way to its core.

Marketing is a challenging pursuit because of scenarios like this one. I've spent my entire professional career advising companies of all shapes and sizes how to walk the marketing path well: how to take a product or a service and expose it to the right buyers at the right time. Most of the work that our agency is approached with, however, has to do with veneer. The focus is on the brochure, the website, and the outdoor creative: the paint job on the car. The view of "marketing" is limited to what colors and fonts to use on the magazine ad instead of what's being advertised (what's under the hood).

I contrast this with other, highly successful brands I encounter that do little or no advertising. Some of the best restaurants in the world don't have to advertise because the product or the experience is so exceptional. I had coffee recently with the owner of Hawkers, an Asian-themed restaurant concept with a handful of highly successful units in the midst of an aggressive expansion. As I learned more and expressed my fascination with his success, he remarked to me that "all of this has come without buying one piece of paid media advertising." Product—not promotion—has driven his growth. Customers still line up out the door.

Some might say that businesses like these don't have to market. I say that they are marketing. They're just playing a game that most aren't familiar with. This line of thinking is not meant to suggest that promotion is not necessary or important, but that promotion is not always the missing link in driving profitability or creating great customer experiences.

In working with a diverse array of clients while being a life-long student of great brands of the world (household names as well as ones most have never heard of), I want to shine a light on the various activities and areas of focus that lay a foundation for what most of our clients are after: a profitable enterprise driven by smart marketing. It is my contention that great marketers are the ones who are successful at developing and blending a number of fairly identifiable elements together to achieve just that.

Whether they know it or not, they are emulating a repeatable recipe—a formula. They are crafting and mixing a cocktail of fairly common things in order to accomplish something extraordinary. One such company, another thriving restaurant brand that has exploded in popularity, headcount, and sales, is 4 Rivers Smokehouse. A homespun barbecue story that quickly took a region by storm, 4 Rivers reflects this thinking with crystal clarity. Founder and CEO, John Rivers, credits his success not to one thing, but the combination of many. "I'm often asked about the one thing that makes 4R successful…is it the brisket, the sauce, or perhaps the people or culture? My answer is yes, plus ten other elements—each equally important—focused in granular detail and incessant intentionality." Either knowingly or unknowingly, thriving brands like 4 Rivers blend multiple things together to create something unique and memorable.

> I'm often asked about the one thing that makes 4R successful… is it the brisket, the sauce, or perhaps the people or culture? My answer is yes, plus ten other elements—each equally important—focused in granular detail and incessant intentionality.
>
> —John Rivers
> Founder and CEO, 4 Rivers Smokehouse

I was inspired to write this book by the most common and challenging questions that marketers face today. In fact, I hear many of these questions from clients we work with and prospects who interview our agency. They are interested in spending money to promote or advertise through everything from billboards on interstates to ads on Facebook but want to know, understandably, what the payoff is. Marketers today, more than ever, want to know how to measure the return of sales they should expect from the dollars they invest in marketing and promotional activities. The question is often asked in retrospect, after a promotional campaign has been launched or completed: Why aren't people buying more? Smart marketers want to know and calculate the return on investment (ROI) of everything they do.

Formulaic answers and addresses this question by challenging the oft-assumed answer to this plea for help: "I need to fix my promotion." The essence of this answer is often wrong. What I keep arriving at is that a client often needs to spend more time worrying about the fundamentals of the business operation, product delivery, or overall experience—the things at the core of the business. In essence, it's a problem with the product—not the promotion. But the promotion is not disconnected from the product—quite the opposite. *Formulaic* argues that there is missing connective tissue between the two, which in many cases prevents businesses from thriving. The promotional activities are disconnected, certainly, from the customer experience, but also from the elements that buttress it: things like how a company hires its people and tells its story and even why it exists. In the way lower back pain can be caused by tightness in one's hamstrings, a lack of sales at the cash register is often caused by other underlying yet connected problems.

This book is about how this process works and how any organization can visualize and emulate it for itself. The book's intent is to serve as both a roadmap of the various aspects of Formulaic thinking (a periodic table of sorts) and an instruction guide (a recipe book, so to speak) for making your own formula. After all, every formula is different. In marketing, one size never fits all.

Consider Coca-Cola, perhaps the most iconic and famous synthetic beverage of all time. It has a very specific formula that is closely guarded in a vault.[1] The same goes for a famous recipe like that of my late grandmother's marinara sauce. She had a very specific formula for crafting what I believe to be the best red sauce ever made—common ingredients available to us all, but only one person in the world who know the specific arrangement, combination, and process required to synthesize it. Or think about the algorithm[2] that Google crafted in order to develop the world's most sophisticated and effective search engine, which literally upended the entire industry and ended almost every competitor; math, science, and logic available to all of us, but only one company crafted a success story that has changed a generation of humanity. Your formula for developing and marketing a business is no different. The aim of this book is to help you find it—and how to be Formulaic in the way you approach your marketing efforts.

This book won't ignore appearances and veneer. After all, a nice paint job and a racing stripe makes all the difference in the world. But in my decades of working with company after company on finding new customers for their products, there's too much weight given to the sizzle over the steak. Marketers tend to spend too much time worrying about the rotating slide show on their website's home page, instead of wrestling with why their customers aren't coming back for a second visit, ordering new services, or referring their friends. That's the stuff that counts.

Formulaic will place more emphasis on ensuring that your marketing "engine" is functioning well, ever improving, and generating more demand for your product or service than you ever thought possible. It's meant for the marketer who is frustrated by reviewing report after report on ad spending and click-through rates and wondering if it's all not just a waste of money.

This book is written for the business owner, the marketer, and anyone inside an organization who wants to see it truly thrive. It's for the person who has the inner feeling that there's great potential for the company they show up to every Monday morning but knows that something's not quite right. It's for the person who is desperate for a recipe to solve the problem.

I've seen this deeper understanding of marketing work, both for our clients and our agency. Our firm has put the elements contained in this book into practice and has enjoyed a multiyear period of growth in revenue, profit, and head count. I think that these ideas—mostly borrowed from best practices and observations of others—can help others. Stated another way, success has patterns.

In addition to smaller companies, I also study the greats. As a student of marketing, I love watching and analyzing the efforts of major advertisers seeking to win the hearts of consumers. I am fascinated by the world's leading brand marketers and how they have succeeded. Brands like Chobani, Lululemon, Bobbi Brown, Patagonia, Apple, Nike, Yeti, Starbucks, and La Croix give me plenty to think about and learn from.

I wrote this book to share the patterns of success that I have witnessed so that brands can get on the right path. I believe that any company can thrive, but not without a deeper look at its core. *Formulaic* will help you start from the inside to evaluate and repair your engine before you even think about the paint job. And in the end, both will work hand in glove to help your brand fly higher than ever.

CHAPTER 1

AN INTRODUCTION TO FORMULAIC THINKING

thrive
/THriv/
Verb
To grow or develop well or vigorously. Prosper; flourish

Formulaic Thinking

You know it when you see it: when you're in a store, a restaurant, a hotel, or the lobby of an architecture firm that's doing extremely well. Perhaps it's the corporate equivalent of an athlete who is "in the zone." You can actually feel it. It's in the décor of the office lobby and in the lighting above the bar. It's in the stylized hand-writing on the chalkboard on the wall of the restaurant and in the way the receptionist looks up from the desk to acknowledge you. It's in how easy the order confirmation e-mail comes to you, along with an easy click-through to the FedEx tracking number.

You see it in the pace of the meal, which is matched to your present need to either get on with your day or unwind for the evening. It's in the meticulous match between the typefaces used on the logo on the door and on the business card. You know when you're in the presence of a business that is leaning forward and bringing others along for the ride. You know when you see a business thriving—killing it.

You also know it when you *don't* see it. You know it when you're in a restaurant where the food is average, the service is weak, and the people working there don't seem to really want to be doing what they're doing. The reviews on social media are average, the decor is blah, the bread is soggy, and the food is lukewarm: the place seems to be running out of gas. You look around and wonder if anyone cares, and then you wonder to yourself, "How long will this place survive?" You can just *feel* when a company is on its last leg and taking its last breath. As a friend of mine likes to say about restaurants that find themselves in that spot, "We should really go give that place another try before it goes out of business."

I decided to write this book because, as the founder of a marketing agency, most businesses I encounter want to be one of those businesses that are indeed prospering or flourishing. Some of them that are already don't even know it and want to tweak things anyway. But most of them approach an agency because they aren't and want to be. They want to thrive.

And that leads me to one of the first common patterns that I see. When most marketers and business owners contemplate marketing, they usually feel like they are missing a particular promotional tactic that would change everything. One tells me his business is not doing well but feels as if a new website will cure his ills. Another tells me that she has no foot traffic but senses that once she hires an intern to start posting pictures on social media, that everything will change for the better. After all, the boutique around the corner is killing it on Instagram. Still another tells me her fitness product would catch on like wildfire if only we could advertise it during the annual January fitness craze that our country seems to embrace after the holidays are over. Most people agree with me that there is no silver bullet when I tell them, but they seem to want to find one anyway. Maybe it's a Facebook ad that will change things. Twitter? Pinterest? Adding more search terms to our site?

Most marketers are inundated with too many promotional ideas and promises. And since everything is measured, the potential for measuring return on investment is pretty obvious. Here is a scenario that I encounter on an almost weekly basis: Client spends $250 on Twitter ads and $500 on Facebook ads to sell a widget. Client then makes a cool spreadsheet to measure the click-throughs, Google Analytics data, and e-commerce reports, only to find that they spent $750 to sell $80 worth of widgets that cost $40 to produce. In other words, they "lost" $710. Client becomes disillusioned with social media spending and moves on to the next tactic.

What's the problem? Ninety-five percent of the time, as an agency observer, this is not a promotional problem. Ironically, though, the client sees promotion as the problem 100 percent of the time. So what's the real problem? The problem is usually somewhere under the hood, not the paint job. Or, as my golf instructor might say, something's wrong with the setup.

The underlying problem could be one of a number of things. Perhaps the widget they are trying to sell, if I'm being candid, is lame, and people don't want to buy it. There's nothing special about it, or perhaps there are ten other widgets that are better. Maybe the widget isn't the type of thing that people want to buy online. Maybe those that buy widgets don't use Twitter or Facebook. It's possible that some of the people went and bought the widget (or a similar widget) on Amazon.com because they're Prime members, and shipping would be free. Perhaps the text or imagery in the ad on Twitter looked like it was produced by a second grader. Or maybe the person doesn't need a widget right now, but might need one later and bought it two weeks later, which was never revealed in the spreadsheet. I could go on and on, but the point of the scenario (which has become all too real and frustrating) is that diagnosing the problem isn't so simple.

As I have traveled and worked with company after company, I've had a front row seat to watch (and be a part of) marketing initiative after marketing initiative. I've also become fascinated with the visible strategies and tactics of thriving marketers and how they do what they do. Whether these brands are pushing yogurt, coffee, cosmetics, or legal services, much can be learned from those companies all around us. As my colleague Kelly likes to say, "Marketing is observation."

Here is what I have come to believe about marketing that I hope to articulate well in this work: successful, thriving businesses don't just excel at clever promotion (that silver bullet that I mentioned earlier). They are able to deeply connect their marketing activities to their core beliefs, values, and ideals in a way that helps them differentiate, resonate, and inspire. In essence, they combine and blend a series of common elements over time into a formula that leads them to that "zone." And while this sounds a bit mystical and ethereal (or like window dressing), I will show you that it's not. I fact, I'll show you that understanding and implementing this Formulaic approach to marketing is essential to your success. Marketing is about the engine, not just the paint job.

I will provide a word of warning, however. Learning the ingredients in the Formula can feel a little disjointed at times. I fully expect that many readers will approach this concept with a certain degree of skepticism. If you find yourself doubtful at times, I would encourage you to press on until the end, when the tie between the fundamentals I prescribe and the success you desire will become readily apparent.

What Choices Have You Made?

I've heard it said that if you look at a business, you can actually trace it back to a decision that someone made—perhaps decades ago—to start it. Most saw a particular need that wasn't being met, had a passion for meeting that need, and took a step forward. And, in most cases, it's a daily choice that someone makes to keep it open. A business that is thriving is driven by that choice. Who made that choice to start your business and why? What drove it? What keeps you going every day?

What Do You Value?

Does your organization know what it values? Think about that for a second. Walmart and Ritz Carlton Hotels are both highly admired companies that are among the most successful in the world. The latter charges twice what its competitors do, while the former charges half. I'm simplifying here, admittedly, but you could say that one values quality regardless of cost, while the other values cost regardless of quality. I happen to be a customer of both—but for very different reasons at different times. Both are unapologetic about what they value, and neither seems to get its wires crossed. Their training, facilities, and customer experience are all aligned around these values—these truths.

The point I'm trying to make is that one value is no better than another, but you must decide what it is your organization values. Without that distinction, you'll never be able to serve, train, or deliver something that echoes in the marketplace. What's worse, you'll always feel pressure to live out (sometimes competing) values.

What's It Like to Work in Your Company?

Given that your company presumably has some established values, how does your company live them out? How do you do things differently? What are the norms, expectations, and "rules" that define what it's like to work in your company? These are all questions that define your organization's culture. Formulaic marketing involves a well-documented culture that is ordained by the company's leadership and reflects the company's values. It is a series of group norms that should be recognizable and distinguishable—they separate your organization from others. This series of guidelines, once formed into a blueprint of some sort, is also a tool that helps you hire and fire. Thriving companies have groups that operate in a unique way, and anything less isn't tolerated.

What's Your Story?

Everyone has a story. Each person, each company, each group has a history and a narrative that explains how it came into formation, why it exists, and why it endures. It also has stories beyond its formation plot that reflect its individuality and unique approach to functioning and why customers should consider it. Beyond just being interesting, storytelling has many scientific benefits. Researchers have empirically proven that storytelling helps listeners connect in a close way with the teller, helps them remember more about the message (as opposed to just hearing facts), and fosters a feeling similar to kindness during the tale. Brands should use the power of storytelling both to build interest and to connect to customers in an intimate way, which builds a relationship and helps them tell their friends about you. Thriving companies have stories to tell—about themselves and about their customers.

How Are You Different?

Is your company unique in some way? Does it stand out? How? The essence of standing out from the crowd is to actually stand out from the crow. I'm being trite, I know. But are you different in clear, tangible ways—big or small? Being different is key and a huge part of what it takes to thrive. Identifying your points of differentiation or what distinguishes you from the rest is fundamental in a Formulaic approach to marketing. And if you can't clearly point them out, it may be time to invent some.

Do You Know Who You Serve?

I have to tell you something that I know you already know. I just want to remind you: you can't make everyone happy. If you're trying, stop. It's OK. I'm giving you permission. You don't have to make everyone happy—just the people you decide you're in business to please. The rest need to take a back seat. Just like Walmart isn't for the bibliophile in search of a rare first edition, and the Ritz-Carlton isn't trying to serve the person looking for a ninety-nine-dollar room. But if you never figure out who you are trying to serve, you'll never stand a chance of truly delighting them. At best, you'll only kind of please some of them some of the time.

What Is It That You Are Selling?

Is your product or service excellent? Do people talk about it to one another and post pictures about it on social media? In many ways, your product *is* your marketing. Companies often mistakenly assume that only the promotional efforts they make represent their marketing. But marketing is more than just promotion. And what you deliver—your widget, your team's approach to service, and the overall experience you provide—is often what carries the day. This is never more apparent than when great brands thrive without any advertising at all; it's simply the product that gives the entire brand the word-of-mouth lift that it needs. Thriving companies sell great things—and keep making new ones.

Are You Willing to Publish?

Marketing is now happening in an age when product discovery, research, and even recommendations mostly happen digitally. Check your Facebook feed. People are using social tools like this to take pictures of their food at the new restaurant they just ate at, rave about the resort they just stayed at for the weekend, talk about the book they read on the beach, and complain about the airline that got them there a couple of hours late. As brands, thriving companies find unique, relevant, and appropriate ways to participate in that exchange, and the currency they use is content that they publish and share. A big part of being Formulaic is developing, publishing, and sharing content of interest and value to your audience through vehicles like blog posts that capture interest in a customer's Facebook feed, instructional videos the might "accidentally" show up in a prospect's Google search, or in a paperback book (similar to the one you are currently holding in your hand) that you decide to write and publish in your area of passion or expertise.

Does Your Promotional Approach Make Sense?

Instead of being sporadic, overly experimental, fad-chasing, or erratic with their promotional efforts, thriving companies typically employ promotional tactics that are sensible, rhythmic, and—most importantly—rooted in the guts of their marketing. That is, the promotion not only asks the masses to buy something, but also invites a very specific audience to enter into a story (over time) in which a unique product experience fits her to a tee and provides value so exceptional that she can't not tell her friends and try it again. Formulaic marketers do all those things at once and perpetuate a cycle of growth like a fertile organism that emerges with the strength and endurance of an oak tree, not the short-lived presence of a mushroom.

Do You Have Patience?

Thriving companies aren't in a hurry. That doesn't mean that they aren't moving fast or don't have a heightened sense of urgency. Quite the contrary. Thriving companies are usually leaning and progressing forward without having unrealistic expectations about when results will materialize. Legendary products and companies are built over decades, not weeks. And like an oak tree takes decades to grow, so does a great, thriving company. Formulaic thinking involves a disposition of steady plotting, consistent effort, discipline, and patience for enduring results to materialize.

Formulaic marketing is about combining, arranging, and blending the answers to these questions into a multipronged, deep-rooted effort to bring lift to your brand. Companies that thrive are able to personalize and refine things like values, story, and culture into a marketing machine—an engine—that makes promotion more natural and reflexive than sporadic. As each of the elements of Formulaic marketing is identified and described, think about how your brand might identify or accentuate each one and blend them together for success. Like the thriving brands described here, you just might find yourself headed toward a new level of prosperity with not just an attractive paint job, but a strong engine as well.

CHAPTER 2

AN ARTICULATED UNDERSTANDING OF WHO YOU ARE

My belief is that companies should have values, like people do.

—Tim Cook, CEO, Apple

In the Atlanta airport, there is a business in terminal A that sells bottles of water, local souvenirs, snacks, travel gadgets, magazines, and a collection of books that lack much of anything distinctive. The store's name? Simply Books. I once went to a sports bar in Orlando that served chicken wings, spaghetti, flatbreads, and a few Thai dishes. None of it was worth eating, mentioning, or ever returning again. The point of this is that these businesses are suffering from an identity crisis: trying to be all things to all people.

A real peril of growing or marketing a business is failing to ponder or commit to an identity. There's nothing wrong with the airport store that wants to sell me a bottle of water, a snack, and a magazine. In fact, it's a good strategy. But flying a flag that says you're simply about a single thing when you do a little bit of everything is *not*.

The marketer who wants to thrive needs to dig deeply. Really deeply. So let's start with what that looks like. The foundation of *Formulaic*—its bedrock—is what lies at the *core* of the brand itself. It has nothing to do with how to write compelling copy for a Twitter ad or how to make a video go viral. The core of the Formula is understanding who you are as a business; articulating it clearly and distinguishably; and for lack of a better term, publishing it—on your wall, on your website, on the back of your employee badges. In other words, figure it out, write it down, and make it known. You must have an articulated understanding of who (as a business) you are at the core.

A thriving brand arrives at who it is at the core by answering challenging questions like the ones above.

Understanding What You Value

As an organization, what do you value? Seriously, what is super important to you? Do you know? Many companies have never stopped to spend much time thinking about values. Inherently, many of them know what they value. In fact, most businesses can agree that quality, for example, is a great thing to value. After all, what kind of business will say that quality isn't important? Or how about customer service? Most would say that customer service is a highly important thing to value.

Because of these commonly held beliefs, many people just glance right over the idea of company values and don't spend too much time with it. After all, we all value pretty much the same things, right? Not really. I can go to a convenience store; a grungy, independent coffee house; Starbucks; and an artisan coffee company that sells a five-dollar pour over, and they all value very different things. One might value convenience, another independence from corporations, and yet another fair trade—yet they all sell coffee. And the nuance among them represents something very distinguishable and strong—a cornerstone or essential component. So what's yours?

I was once in the Houston airport on a layover and needed to grab a quick sandwich before my next flight. I noticed a Subway restaurant and quickly jumped in line. I'd been to many different Subway locations over the years, but this particular location was different. Instead of one or two "sandwich artists" behind the line, there must have been six. As I ordered my sandwich and made my bread choice, the first person sprang into action quickly. Before I took a step, the sandwich was down the line being prepared. One team member after another rushed me down the line, as I hustled just to keep up. I struggled to keep pace with the options and my selections. Before I knew it, my sandwich was in a bag, and the cashier was waiting for my credit card. I almost felt guilty for being slow or that I was letting them down! When I got to the end of the line, I exchanged a laugh with the manager standing there. When I asked him what that was all about, he simply replied, "This Subway serves more sandwiches than any other location in the world. Our customers can't afford to wait." It was clear what this particular business valued: speed.

Compare that scenario with the internationally recognized pop culture icon, the Soup Nazi. Yev Kassem, the chef and entrepreneur on whom the television character was based, was known to serve New Yorkers different varieties of soup that were so original, tasty, and noteworthy that customers lined up around the corner and waited in the cold for his famous soup.[3] There was no place to sit, and the location was almost shabby in comparison to other nearby restaurants. The soup was so good, and the demand was so high, though, that Kassem posted some signs around the cash register, discouraging small talk and pleasantries and goading customers to have their payment ready quickly. The terse soup chef caught the attention of comedian and actor Jerry Seinfeld, who portrayed the famous chef in a humorous light by illuminating his almost dismissive approach to business. The business was a phenomenon for many years by valuing one thing: product excellence.

Another example of values in action is Southwest Airlines, which places a great degree of emphasis on the value of fun. If you have a choice of airlines and want a quiet ride to get some sleep or enjoy some peace and quiet, don't choose Southwest! Almost every flight is meant for fun. Flight attendants are known to sing the federally mandated announcements or poke fun at one another during the trip. I've been on flights on which the flight attendants encourage passengers to use the call buttons to serve as "buzzers" for trivia games. Even the pilot crew is known to get in on the action by cracking jokes before and after takeoff. Southwest values fun, and it shows.[4]

If you walk into a Wells Fargo bank branch anywhere, you see very prominently what the organization values: courtesy. Behind every customer service counter in every branch is a prominent quote from founder Henry Fargo in 1874: "We have one very powerful business rule. It is concentrated into one word: courtesy." It doesn't say it all (there's no mention of security, convenience, professionalism, etc.), but it says enough. It is a central nexus to let us all know what the company is about.

Determining Why You Do What You Do

When author and speaker Simon Sinek went to deliver a TED talk (the same forum that had previously been addressed by the likes of Bill Gates, President Bill Clinton, and Richard Branson) to a crowd of eager listeners, no one knew that he was about to give one of the most popular TED talks of all time. His presentation has been viewed tens of millions of times, and his book on the same subject struck a nerve in the business community the ripples of which are still being felt. The focus of his work centered around a simple word: *why*.[5]

Sinek's admonition to leaders, in essence, is to figure out why your business exists as a means of revealing or illuminating its core purpose or spirit, independent of what it does. His primary example is Apple. Apple, he explains, makes computers (the what) but does it to change the status quo (the why). Knowing and understanding why you exist is critical to amplifying your values, galvanizing the spirit of your company, and flying a flag around which both customers and employees might rally.

As an agency, we develop strategies, create names for products, develop websites, and do a host of other things that other agencies might do—the what. But after twenty years, that's not what gets me out of bed in the morning. What does is our why. We exist because we see a great benefit to our world in connecting customers who need good things with those who have a dream of satisfying those needs (our clients). When we help the entrepreneur or executive with a passion empower or improve the lives of others or help a social services organization find ways to better meet the needs of their clients, we are fulfilled in a way that transcends money.

We were fighting against conformity, against boringness, against drudgery. More than a product, we were trying to sell an idea—a spirit.

— Phil Knight
Founder, Nike

Imagine if a church or synagogue existed merely to dispense liturgy or literature to people (the what) without any compassion or drive to enrich lives or to alleviate suffering (the why). That would render that institution soulless. In this same way, you as a marketing firm must define and draw out your collective soul. Great companies have souls. As Phil Knight, founder of Nike, explains in his memoir, "We were fighting against conformity, against boringness, against drudgery. More than a product, we were trying to sell an idea—a spirit.[6]" Great companies have a defined spirit, soul, or higher calling. They have a heartbeat. What's yours?

Going Soul Searching

Understanding what your company values and why it exists is the job of leadership. If a company is just starting up, there's often a reason that drove the decision to start the business. It could be as benign as simply inventing a better mousetrap than the next guy. Or perhaps the company has been in existence for some time. In any case, leadership must invest the time in understanding what it values, why it exists, and so on.

Understanding things like values and conceptual drivers of why the organization exists involves leadership designating time to do so. This can happen along the way, as a company evolves or when it hits an inflection point and decides it needs to dedicate time to doing so. It can be meeting time that is programmed (sometimes in the form of an off-site meeting or retreat) or developed along the way. This type of thinking and reflection typically doesn't happen overnight—it happens over time, usually when the pulls and stresses of the day-to-day activities aren't present. Thinking like this happens in the shower, sitting by the lake, driving to the grocery store, during a long flight, or any other time when you're away from the office. The bottom line is that an organization must create or leverage time to search for its soul.

Some good questions to guide a leader or leadership team along this process are as follows:

- Why do we exist?
- What do we want to be best in the world at?
- Why did this organization begin?
- What do we aspire to be?
- When they write our history in twenty-five years, what will have been our story?
- What do we value that our chief competitors seem to ignore?
- Beyond our product, what impact are we looking to make on the world?

Articulating Who You Are

It's not enough to simply go searching for an organizational soul; the organization must document it. If a leadership team agrees on what an organization is about conceptually, it's not enough to simply nod your heads and talk about it regularly. Why? Because details get lost. Turnover happens, and people forget. Words and meanings get twisted. Over time, the message gets diluted and can eventually evaporate. Documentation can help memorialize the message and ultimately institutionalize it. Once that happens, the opportunity for those values to actually mean something practically can help.

There are lots of ways to document the conceptual soul of a company. And while not all of these are necessary, they are all helpful in some respect.

Statement of Values

What an organization values should be written down. While most organizations value many, many things, it is useful to narrow them down to a concise list, so the focus of the organization is clear. The simpler the list is, the easier it is to remember.

It is also helpful to frame these values in unique ways to put your own stamp on them. In other words, don't just use vague terms like *customer service* and *quality*. Consider phraseology that is memorable. For example, Nemours Children's Hospital frames values[7] such as "have courageous conversations" and "be in the moment." Cloud-storage company Dropbox, which limits its list to only five for the sake of simplicity, encourages team members to "be worthy of trust" and "sweat the details." Its fifth and final value is simply a smiley face on a cupcake![8] Give it some personality.

Vision Statement

Does your company have a vision? A vision is a brief statement that describes your organization's picture of a preferred future—an articulation of a collective destination. It's usually a single sentence. Microsoft's founding vision was "a desktop computer on every desk in every home and every office."[9] A local homeless organization might state its vision as "a community where every citizen has a meal and a bed every day of every year." It simply creates a dot on the horizon that lets employees, customers, and other stakeholders know where the organization is headed one day in the (usually distant) future.

Mission Statement

Your company's mission statement is just that: your statement that you're on a mission to do something. A mission is a big, bold articulation of the purpose you hope to serve. Like a James Bond movie, it implies that there is risk, tension, and a clear indication of purpose.

Company mission statements are often the essence of strategy and imply action and direction. While they can be quite lengthy, management professor Jim Collins, author of *Good to Great*, encourages leaders to make them brief and memorable. Collins believes they should be able to fit on the front of a t-shirt. They should inspire, connect, and move stakeholders. The Starbucks mission statement is a great example: "to inspire and nurture the human spirit—one person, one cup, and one neighborhood at a time."

Starbucks Mission

To inspire and nurture the human spirit—one person, one cup, and one neighborhood at a time.

Painted Picture

Another way to articulate the vision of your brand is called the painted picture. It is the result or output of a company visioning exercise outlined in the book *Double Double: How to Double Your Revenue and Profit in Three Years or Less*, by Cameron Herold. Our agency went through the exercise outlined in the book, and our painted picture helped us double revenue and profit in three years.

Essentially, the process involves you "painting a picture" of what your company needs to look like three years down the road. It forces you to think (or dream, really) about how many customers you will have, how much revenue will exist, how many employees will comprise the team, even what awards you will have won. It should reflect drastic differences between where your business is now and where you want it to be. Herold encourages readers to share it with employees, customers, and even the media to build momentum toward a different station in the company's life. It is aspirational, inspirational, and motivational to all involved. It reflects the company's soul and future.

Brand Mirror

Another document or exercise that can be helpful is something called a brand mirror. It was conceived by my longtime colleague and fellow principal in our agency, Kelly Lafferman. The exercise and output challenge leaders to write what they would see in a mirror if they were to hold it up to the brand. It can address many areas, but it gives internal stakeholders an idea of what the brand feels like. It answers questions like these:

- If our brand was a celebrity, who would it be?
- What is on our brand's Spotify playlist?
- What does our brand do after work and on weekends?
- How does our brand speak? Are we funny, formal, serious, or curt?
- What does our brand wear to work?
- What's our brand's favorite cocktail?

The resulting document gives the reader a feel for what the personality of the brand is. Along these lines, it also personifies the brand and establishes its voice. After all, your brand should have a distinctive voice. It's particularly helpful to new employees who seek to understand the essence of the brand persona and helps them think, speak, and act as one unit, without sacrificing team-member individuality, of course. It simply guides creative choices when writing copy for a web page or a social media post.

As your company's leadership goes soul searching, it must articulate and document its findings and put them on display in the appropriate fashion. A mission statement, for example, needs to be known by everyone inside and around the company. Making this happen means creating documents and other touch points for people to learn, understand, remember, and leverage the soul of the organization. Different ideas include printed documents, wallet-size cards, signs on walls, digital displays, and videos. The bottom line is that your brand needs to understand who it is (along with who it's not) and articulate it to itself and the world.

Formulaic marketing begins with a rundown of who you are as a brand. Companies that thrive are usually very sure of this: what they value, why they do what they do, and how they want to do it. They've completed the hard work of getting to the heart—the core—of who their brand is. And they're often outspoken and unapologetic about it all. As we will learn in subsequent chapters, thriving brands aren't trying to please absolutely everyone anyway. They're simply trying to be the absolute best for those they intend to serve.

CHAPTER 3

A DEFINED CULTURE

> Culture eats strategy for breakfast.
>
> —Peter Drucker

What Is Culture?

As I travel from company to company—or even country to country—it becomes clear to me that culture is a misunderstood term. A "culture" isn't a place, and it isn't the idea that laughing at the office makes for a "great culture." Too many people assume that culture is about fun because that's so often what is revered in workplace culture. The singing flight attendants at Southwest Airlines are a good example. While culture can include fun, laughter, and positive reinforcement, that's not necessarily what culture is.

Culture is about expectations, norms, rules, and a shared understanding. Culture is about a common agreement concerning how we operate, how we roll, how we do things here. It's about creating a framework for *how* we will do things that we all agree to.

Considering a four-way stop while driving is a helpful way to understand culture. When you ease into a stop at a four-way intersection, each of which is marked with a red stop sign, you are experiencing culture. If you are an experienced driver, you know that your turn to proceed from a full stop comes when the other three who came to a stop before you have moved forward. No driver gestures, flashes his or her high beams, or acts confused. The culture of a four-way stop is to come to a complete stop, and only proceed when it's your turn. We do it without thinking because we understand this is what the rules dictate in that environment.

Companies have these nuances within them whether they know it or not. The Southwest Airlines example of fun is one that most of us have seen and felt. Contrast that with the culture of the Navy SEALs, in which fun has very little to do with how they train and operate. There, the *how* is about intensity, perseverance, and undying focus on teamwork and loyalty. The Ritz-Carlton has identifiable habits of over-the-top service that it rolls into a package called "Gold Standards."[10] Ask one of their "ladies and gentlemen" how to get to the fitness center, and he or she won't tell you how to get there; you will be escorted to the entrance personally. Culture is about the little decisions like these that you make about how you will operate.

Why Is Culture Important?

As you understand what culture is, it is important to absorb that culture is important. This book has talked about the importance of defining *who* you are (and who you are not). We've also echoed Simon Sinek's famous TED talk, which explains that *why* your brand exists is critical, in terms of building and reinforcing meaning and purpose. Culture is about the *how*.

If your company is an engine, think of culture as the lubrication that makes all the parts work together. It provides flow, movement, and protection for the hardworking parts of the engine. It minimizes friction and fosters motion.

Your Culture Needs a Blueprint

Whether you know it or not, your company already has a culture. Culture happens in some form or fashion, the same way that water finds low spots during a flood. No one tells the water where to go—it just goes.

Here's something to observe the next day you go to work. When the company opens its doors in the morning and is officially open for business, is everyone sitting at their chairs doing work, or do people wander in over the course of the next thirty minutes? Some companies are very lax about time, while others are very firm.

Celebrity chef Anthony Bourdain is an instructive example to consider. He sees "enforcing arrival time as the most important way to set the tone and reinforce the understanding that [he gives] the orders." Bourdain fires an employee on his or her second offense of being tardy.[11]

> Enforcing arrival time [is] the most important way to set the tone and reinforce the understanding that [I] give the orders.
>
> — Anthony Bourdain

Bourdain's rigidity with respect to time is not for everyone, but his approach to structure, reinforcement, and boundary setting is instructional for us all. That's why some characterize and define culture as "the least acceptable behavior that you will tolerate." If Chef Bourdain chooses to tolerate the absence of a behavior that is important to him, the rule loses its strength to influence the organization. The rule becomes, then, a mere suggestion. The expected behavior of the team then evaporates. The culture has become diluted.

For Bourdain, it's about punctuality. For Southwest, it's about fun. For the speedy Subway restaurant in the Houston Airport mentioned in the previous chapter, what is it that you want your brand to be about that can be influenced by the culture? Only your vision of the experience you are trying to cultivate will do that.

No one culture is right; it is about deciding what is right for you. Culture can certainly be nuanced, but it's possible to define the nuance and provide clarity. You must define and articulate the culture so that it can be memorialized, talked about, and institutionalized. This makes it more tangible and real.

To prevent your culture from forming like floodwaters flow on their own, you must define the behaviors—the *hows*—that represent the heart of your culture. You must literally look for, identify, and document the various behaviors that you'd like to see acted out and repeated.

Facebook gives employees a small handbook that it calls *The Little Red Book*.[12] It lays out a number of different cultural ideals and cheers like "The Quick Shall Inherit the Earth," which encourages speed in launching new products. Zappos also publishes a book about its culture, in which it encourages ideals like humility and doing more with less.[13] But you don't necessarily have to publish a book. You could develop a simple list of norms, ideals, or rules and put it on your website and on your wall.

Nemours Children's Health System does that very thing and lists behaviors like "Volunteer Discretionary Effort Constantly" and "Look in the Mirror First—Be Accountable" on the back of its employee badges and in other prominent places throughout its many facilities. Whether you write a book, produce a video, or develop a list, every brand needs a codified document or blueprint that encapsulates the type of culture you wish to build.

Building from the Blueprint

Once you know how you want to define your culture, the next step is in building and reinforcing its elements. Brands need leaders who will find ways to take the facets of the culture and make them real. There are many ways to do this, but here are a few tangible ways to build the culture through reinforcement:

- Role modeling—If your cultural design contains behaviors and rules that leaders can model, then they must be the ones out front, walking the walk for others to see.
- Displays—If the tenets of the culture aren't written down and on display, they will be forgotten. True, hanging them on the wall is not enough, but it's a start.
- Symbols and artifacts—Like any global culture, corporate cultures can have artifacts as well. Common artifacts in a company culture might include portraits of founders, pictures of important company events, framed notes from customers, and other physical objects. One company I once worked with used the green apple as a symbol of staying current and ever growing.
- Rituals—A ritual is a simple activity or exercise that you repeat from time to time to reinforce the rules or behaviors you wish to keep top of mind. The Ritz-Carlton has a lineup every morning, during which all employees assemble and discuss one of the company's cultural tenets.
- Rewards—You can reinforce your team's culture-friendly behaviors by catching employees in the act, acknowledging their act(s), and publicly praising or rewarding them for it.
- Language and lexicon—What you say and how you say it are also a part of your company's culture. Commonly used phrases, words, and nicknames help separate your culture from that of others. I once toured the large, established Miller Brewing Company in Milwaukee, whose presentation was institutional and corporate, while the younger, smaller Milwaukee Brewing Company's brewery tour included brash remarks and sophomoric language. Words alone represented a clear difference in culture.
- Celebrations and events—It's your brand, so there is nothing stopping you from injecting some celebration(s) or

event(s) into the company's schedule to routinely talk about and reinforce the culture. Quality expert Philip B. Crosby used to recommend that companies interested in perpetuating a quality mind-set within their cultures should hold an annual celebration day to revisit the purpose and importance of a focus quality.

What's This Got to Do with Marketing?

If you're reading all this and thinking to yourself, "Hey wait, I thought I was reading a book about how to sell more stuff, not some feel-good HR treatise," let me explain. Culture has everything to do with marketing.

Culture is a way to differentiate your product. It's also a way to shape the experience your customer has because of some things that you've chosen to do differently than your competitors. Ultimately, this can lead to something remarkable that defines you and encourages your customers to tell others about their experience. Singing flight attendants might not be for you, but they certainly shape a fun experience for many people. And that is often worth talking about. You couldn't breed that type of atmosphere and hire that type of person (not everyone likes to sing, you know) if your culture didn't permit and encourage it.

> Culture is a way to differentiate your product. It's also a way to shape the experience your customer has because of some things that you've chosen to do differently than your competitors.

Outdoor apparel and equipment company Patagonia has enjoyed decades of global success, credited in large part to its cultural blueprint, which founder Yvon Chouinard refers to as "the philosophies."[14] According to him, having the philosophies in writing has played a critical role in the success of the company, especially through more difficult times. If there is a thriving brand to emulate over the past fifty years, you would be hard pressed to find one more compelling than Patagonia.

If the product experience you are going for is fast and minimizes waiting, then the behavior of your people certainly ought to reflect that. If you want your buyers or visitors to feel welcomed, acknowledged, and appreciated, then your culture ought to hire and cultivate those types of personalities.

In this sense, you can think of culture as a bridge between what you value and what you actually deliver. One of our agency's clients is a New Orleans boutique specifically for plus-size women called Jaci Blue. Founder Jaclyn McCabe's internal admonition to her employees—and noted ingredient in her success—is to "never make the fat girl feel fat in the fat girl store." Jaclyn is quick to note that the word "fat" is one that she, "along with several women in the plus-size community, verbalize as our own way to take the emotional charge out of the stigma." She encourages employees to recognize and highlight the beauty of every customer who enters. How the employees carry this out each day is a part of the experience, just as important as the clothes Jaci Blue sells.

Culture is the incubator for the experience your customer has with your product. In essence, culture is a huge part of marketing.

Hiring and Firing

As the Anthony Bourdain example suggests, a culture is only as good as the team's acceptance and embodiment of it. As you consider your culture and the components of its blueprint, your people's personalities, traits, and tendencies must fit within it.

When you look at hiring new people and bringing them into the organization, your cultural blueprint should be a lens through which you evaluate them. You must certainly look at the skills and experience that the candidate might bring to the job, but you must also evaluate him or her in terms of your culture. Quite simply, you must ask yourself when hiring if he or she will "fit." Will he or she be willing to do things the way you want them done? It is advisable to talk about your cultural tenets during the interview process and even post them in the recruiting and hiring section of your website.

One of our agency's clients, an investment management firm, uses a "cultural screener" to gauge a fit between the tenets of the company culture and the behaviors of the candidates it is interviewing. The screener is a series of questions to contemplate and consider about a candidate's norms, values, and beliefs.

One of the devices that Google uses when hiring is something called the LAX test to gauge how interesting, collegial, and intellectually stimulating a person is.[15] The LAX test asks an interviewer to consider whether he or she would be able to handle being stuck on a six-hour layover at the Los Angeles International Airport (also known as LAX) with the person.

Consider Strand Bookstore near Union Square Park in New York City. Strand, boasting "eighteen miles of books," has been an outlier in the book industry. In a world where physical bookstores are an endangered species due to e-readers and online booksellers like Amazon.com, Strand has thrived. The store has about two hundred employees, moves about 2.5 million books per year, and sells rare books for as much as forty-five thousand dollars. Its secret? How it selects its people.

Strand only hires people who live, breathe, and think about the world of books and reading. Customers who ask an employee of the store about a book or reading are likely to not only be shown where a book is or how to find it, but to be enthusiastically assisted, surprised by a recommendation, or encouraged by a "That's a great book" comment. Why? Because all employees of Strand are required to pass a test, referred to in retail circles as "the quiz." Strand applicants are required to pass a brief quiz on books, authors, and genres to test their enthusiasm for reading. Only about two of every sixty applicants are hired. The quiz helps

Strand managers hire passionate people, who make for remarkable customer experiences.[16]

I visited Strand to get a sense of the place. When you do visit it, you feel the difference in the conversations and interactions with the employees. They're book people, and you can tell. In asking one of them about the quiz, I got a wry smile and a chuckle. "It's true that there is a quiz," one employee told me, "but it's easy." Easy for you, I thought to myself, but not for the other fifty-eight applicants who weren't hired.

As new employees arrive or current ones are asked to modify how they do things within the company, your cultural blueprint should be used to coach and manage employees as they work. Culture is important, so management should look for opportunities to build culture as they perform. Ultimately, team members who refuse to acknowledge the importance of culture (and certainly those who flat out reject it) might be doing more harm than good to the organization. Their refusal to build culture, as discussed before, may have a negative impact on the customer's experience. They are likely a better fit for a different organization with a different culture.

Where to Start

Admittedly, defining your cultural elements and developing a blueprint are challenging tasks. It's not easy to make decisions about how you want an organization to behave, to look, and to feel. Part of the difficulty is that there is no singular right answer, no way to encapsulate every behavior that you want to see, and there's plenty of nuance.

For starters, engage others in the process. The more you can engage others in defining the proper aspects of the culture, the more they will be invested in the outcomes, and the greater ownership they will feel. Ultimately, having multiple people own the culture is a positive thing. Buy in from others is important.

Second, consider the definition of your culture to be a long-term process. You must observe behaviors over time, not in an hour-long session or half-day retreat. It takes time to tease out the various rules and behaviors you'd like to perpetuate. So remember to be patient with yourself and your team.

Once you're ready to embark on the process of formulating your cultural blueprint, you can start with a few questions. While your brainstorming and formulation might be far more wide ranging, the following questions can help you get the conversation going:

- What are the little things that make us tick?
- What words and phrases are unique to us?
- What clichés are we particularly fond of?
- What do we all seem to laugh at together?
- What behaviors do we encourage or would we like to see more of?
- What geographic locations or architectural icons are important to us?
- What do we not tolerate?
- What famous leaders, inventors, athletes, or other heroes do we admire?
- Who are our folk heroes whose spirits seem to inspire us?
- What physical objects would you see in our office that you wouldn't see in other places?
- If we built a time capsule, what would we put in it?
- What common threads run through the people who comprise the heart and soul of our brand?
- What do our founders or leaders do to set the tone?
- What do we insist on in our organization?
- What are deal breakers for us when hiring new people?
- What would customers say in terms of what it feels like to work with us?

Once you have put these thoughts and ideas together on your organization's behalf, use the voice of your brand to phrase them.

How you phrase the elements of your culture is just as important as what they consist of. Ritz-Carlton uses phraseology like "anticipation and compliance with guest needs" while Crispin Porter + Bogusly, an advertising agency, encourages employees not to "talk shit" or "play the busy card." Both are correct, because their wording helps to amplify the culture.[17] And as a rule of thumb, focus on specific behaviors you'd like to see (e.g., bend over backward for the customer in front of you), not broad terms or ideals (e.g., customer service).

Figuring out how you want to do things is just as important as what you do. Perhaps you've already determined this but simply need to write it down for others. Or perhaps you have written it down but just need to reinforce it more often or use it to hone the composition of your team. Wherever you may find yourself with your culture, it is important to recognize that it's a major part of the engine that drives thriving companies to success. Formulaic marketing emanates from the inside, not the outside, and how you do things (differently) is part and parcel of the heart and soul of your company.

CHAPTER 4

A STORY TO TELL

> Man is a storytelling animal. He is a teller of stories that aspire to truth.
>
> —Alasdair Macintyre

One of the first jobs I ever held was during the height of the movie-rental industry, when Netflix was still just a dream. I worked at a locally owned video rental business that grew quickly and thrived in Central Florida called 16,000 Movies. This little upstart company rose quickly at a time when Blockbuster Video was all the rage across the country and seemingly held a monopoly in almost every city in America—except Orlando, Florida. Rumor had it that Blockbuster tried to buy the 16,000 several times because of its success in Central Florida.

Not only did the company own and rent thousands of tapes weekly—it did so in an atmosphere that evolved into a local hangout for movie buffs, families, and local high-school students looking to pass the time on weekends. The company gave away free popcorn and allowed you to reserve movies to be sure you could see new releases. Somehow, the place had evolved into a place to see and be seen with tons of energy, laughter, and community. It was the first truly thriving company I had ever seen from the inside.

So how did one local company emerge to be a David to the Goliath that was Blockbuster? It all started with a little story that turned into a legend. What motivated founder Robert Zlatkiss to start the company was a trip he once took to would-be rival Blockbuster Video to rent a copy of *Star Wars*. He walked into the quiet store and noticed that two employees behind the counter didn't even bother to say hello to him as he entered. He made his way over to the "Action and Adventure" section to find his movie but couldn't. He walked over to the counter to ask for assistance. The two clerks, who couldn't be bothered to take a break from twiddling their thumbs, gave him a couple of vague instructions on the location of the film and gestured in the general direction of a particular shelf. Zlatkiss walked over once again, failed to find the movie, and proceeded to walk out. We can only assume that the clerks couldn't even be bothered to say good-bye. It was then and there that Blockbuster gave birth to its soon-to-be rival.

There were many elements involved in the success of the 16,000 Movies chain. Elements like selection, free popcorn, and a friendly staff all played a part. But it was the company's story that became the driving force for employees to go above and beyond to help each and every customer and to keep each one coming back for more. Employees were encouraged to use this story as a rally cry for friendliness and over-the-top customer service.

As seen in the Formulaic marketing of other thriving brands, stories are brand messengers of the highest form. Blended with elements like documented values and a cultural blueprint, stories play a critical role in communicating a company's identity and purpose to both its team members and its customers with a high level of impact. Thriving brands tell stories that connect, resonate, and imprint a memorable message in the hearts and minds of the listener. Part of a successful approach to Formulaic marketing is recognizing those stories, recording them, and telling them to those who care to listen.

Storytelling as a Marketing Device

Growing up, one of my favorite times of the year was when my maternal grandmother would visit us during the holidays. Before bed, she would always get the kids together and tell us stories. My siblings and I would hang on every word. There were stories of cops and robbers, ghost stories, and even a story about a school of porpoises saving her from a shark. To this day, more than thirty years later, I still remember many of them.

Stories can be fictional, and stories can be factual. Either way, they're very powerful. Stories and oral tradition are how our cultures and societies have formed—long before pencil and paper, and certainly long before Snapchat. Without story, we would have very little history.

Steve Jobs knew this. When asked to give a commencement address to the graduating class at Stanford University, he did it by simply telling three stories.[18] If you haven't already, you should watch his speech on YouTube. Trust me when I tell you that it's worth your time.

Aside from the anecdotal evidence, research supports the notion that authentic storytelling (not my grandmother's variety) helps consumers feel closer to a brand. According to some research highlighted in *Psychology Today*, buyers prefer emotion to data and respond in greater magnitude in this respect. Said differently, stories about facts are more powerful than facts alone.

> Buyers prefer emotion to data.
>
> — Psychology Today

One example that comes to mind comes from the assisted-living industry. This industry seeks to help adult children who are caring for aging parents. For the adult children, it's a scary time and one during which they seek assurance about safety, personalized caregiving, and quality of life.

As a marketer, Brookdale Senior Living could very easily just put these facets on a web page or in a brochure and call it a day: "Brookdale works hard to ensure safety, deliver personalized caregiving, and promote a high quality of life for your loved ones." But that would be lazy and boring, and it would look just like all its competitors.

In its television advertising campaign, the company says very little about itself—about how caring it is, how safety conscious it is, or how it personalizes the care it provides. The employees simply tell stories about the special connections they have made with its residents. In listening to the stories, prospects get a palpable sense of how those who work at Brookdale view their jobs as less of a vocation and more of a calling.

> Our branding philosophy is to tell people who we are.
>
> — Yvon Chounard
> Founder, Patagonia

Patagonia, a leading outdoor apparel company, tells stories to its customers that are written by its customers about its customers. Its catalog comprises photos and stories that its customers submit regularly about adventures and expeditions that most often involve the apparel and equipment in action. This fits well with the company's unique branding philosophy: "tell people who we are."[19] Its customers' stories are the currency of that effort.

The Science behind Storytelling

When we think about the word *storytelling*, it harkens back to our childhood, when a parent, grandparent, or other adult in our lives entertained or taught us through stories. We don't often associate storytelling with strategic marketing. But think about it the next time you catch yourself listening to a story that a friend or loved one is telling you. It feels different—either engaging, intimate, or otherwise emotional. For those reasons, there is a nostalgia and ingrained positive feeling associated with stories. Consider that the next time a friend or loved one begins a sentence with "I have to tell you a story." Better yet, notice how engaged you become when a speaker at a podium leads with a story. If you're like me, you will notice that it gets your juices flowing a bit more than facts or an ill-timed joke.

But science has gone further to give us a glimpse of how and why stories are such powerful communication devices. By measuring and analyzing brain activity, researchers have proven that we process facts and stories quite differently. For example, when someone tells a story about a concept and someone else recites facts, your brain handles the information differently and even uses different parts of the brain to do so. When one person tells a story to another, part of the phenomenon that occurs is the production of a chemical in the brain called oxytocin, the same substance that materializes when we are trusted and shown kindness.[20] When we tell stories, we engender intimacy, trust, and positive feelings.

Beyond good feelings, we build true connections with others. Brain wave activity research by Princeton professor and neuroscientist Uri Hasson has proven that the brains of both the storyteller and listener actually "sync" during a story. "By simply telling a story," Professor Hasson explains, "[a storyteller] can actually plant ideas, thoughts, and emotions into the listeners' brains."[21]

> Great stories are easily recalled, due to the power of their sensory associations.
>
> — Robert Snyder
> Johns Hopkins University

A further, yet perhaps most important, effect of storytelling has to do with deep and profound recall. Listeners remember stories better than they do facts. While facts on a PowerPoint slide or handout are certainly clear and understandable, they're tough for us to memorize or recall. Because storytelling activates a different part of our brains and a seemingly separate processing methodology, "great stories are easily recalled, due to the power of their sensory associations," according to Johns Hopkins researcher and neuroscientist Robert Snyder.[22] In other words, if you want someone to remember something more easily, tell them a story.

What's Your Story?

Just like people, brands have stories. And in order to connect, build goodwill, and foster memorability, they should figure out what they are and tell them.

Telling a story doesn't imply that the message is fictional—although many great stories are. Story simply involves communicating something that happened in a way that is interesting, exciting, and engaging.

Great stories often have common structure and elements. As you contemplate your brand's stories, you can leverage these components to ensure that your story truly resonates with the listener. While no two stories have the exact same structure, some of those common elements are as follows:

- Setting—To tell a story that resonates, you have to set the stage. The content of your story is important, but the setting provides context, which helps to frame and shape your story's events and message. As you begin to describe your story, shape the scene so listeners can relate. Tell us where the story takes place, what the weather was like, and the time and era with respect to historical events. Explain the mood of the environment and other general details to help listeners visualize and truly understand the backdrop.
- Characters—Great stories have character profiles that are interesting, developed, and multidimensional. Think about

and illuminate characters by describing personality, physical appearance, tendencies, histories, and anything else that makes them unique. Characters represent people, and listeners connect and bond unknowingly with them. Also, we often find ourselves rooting for or against particular characters, based on their dispositions or their relationships with us.

- Conflict—Stories that resonate with us have characters or circumstances that create drama, tension, or a sense that diametric forces are colliding. The conflict itself can also generate an emotional feeling within us when we listen to it unfold. Conflict can make us bury our faces in our hands, jump in our seats, or cringe and look away. That emotional reaction creates a feeling within us that is hard to forget and often makes the stories memorable. Your story should describe the conflict(s) you or your customers have faced.

- Connection—A brand story with impact also connects with the audience. This element helps the listener to empathize, because he or she can insert him- or herself into the storyline in some way. Connection is "the bridge between the audience and your organization," according to nonprofit storytelling expert Christopher Davenport, author of *Nonprofit Storytelling for Board Members*, who encourages nonprofits to appeal to listener desires for things like "a clean environment to live in, safe neighborhoods, loving, families, etc… When we engage the audience on…basic levels, they are saying, 'I have that same want/desire/need.'"

- Memorable moments—Great stories that we remember or find ourselves repeating often have aspects or dynamics that are funny, scary, or fantastic in some way. These can be funny quotes, odd behavior, or unbelievable circumstances. Nike founder Phil Knight described how his partner and Oregon track coach Bill Bowerman used to experiment with soles of shoes by pouring liquid rubber into his wife's waffle iron to create the patterns he envisioned. Farmers Insurance tells true stories of claims they have received and satisfied that are truly remarkable. Its "hall of claims" features a homeowner who improperly installed a water heater, which became so pressurized, it rocketed through the roof and landed on a car parked in front of the home. If your story had some incredible details, make sure they are recorded and included.

- Vulnerability—As you think about telling a story about your brand, you will likely feel compelled to describe characters and events in a positive light. After all, you want listeners to think positively about your brand and see it as a hero and a victor. While this is certainly natural, it is key that you convey an air of vulnerability, so you properly frame a success or triumph. Every *Rocky* movie, for example, features a victory at the end, but only after a series of prior failures on the part of the protagonist. Vulnerability is not weakness or fallibility—it's a way to make a story genuine. In the words of storytelling expert and genre advocate Catherine Burns, "the number one quality of great storytellers is their willingness to be vulnerable, their ability to tell on themselves."

These and other elements can help you form good stories that truly connect and help your message to travel. You can choose to tell all types of stories about your brand. For starters, tell the story about why and how your company or organization got started. It's a big one to think about, develop, and repeat and highly important in a variety of ways. Professor Paul Zak calls this type of story a "founding myth" and describes it as "an effective way to communicate transcendent purpose by sharing [it]." These stories, "repeated over and over, stay core to the organization's DNA" and "provide guidance for daily decision making as well as the motivation that comes with conviction that the organization's work must go on, and needs everyone's full engagement to make a difference in people's lives."

> The number one quality of great storytellers is their willingness to be vulnerable, their ability to tell on themselves.
>
> — Catherine Burns

You can also tell stories about individual customers and their triumphs in partnership with you. The Farmers Insurance story previously mentioned is a great example of how incredible (and hard to believe) life circumstances are met with strength and responsiveness by the company. Arnold Palmer Children's Hospital is featured in a story called the "Thank You Project," in which the mother of a child whose life was saved by the team at the hospital returns ten years later to thank the team individually and throw them a party. The story was not only true, it was incredibly powerful and was propelled all the way to a feature on the *Today* show around Thanksgiving Day.

Stories matter, and they also travel well. Begin documenting them and sharing them, so your brand can be lifted high. Recording and retelling great stories about your brand can help people understand why you exist and show them how you are different, based on things that have actually happened. Your stories will help your brand connect with others, engender feelings of closeness, and help them remember you. And since stories travel well, creating and perpetuating them.

Formulaic marketing is about blending things like values and culture and communicating about them to the world through the experience you deliver to the customer. And one of the best ways to communicate what's at the core of your brand—to describe the engine that drives you—is by telling stories. Stories can come in all forms and facets, make you laugh or bring you to tears, and communicate why it is you do what you do. And thriving brands collect and repeat stories to others to showcase what they do and why they do it in ways that build connections with customers, help them remember, and position them to tell others. So tell your story truthfully and layer in some vulnerability to make it stick. You'll soon discover that the stories you tell can have far more impact than the cleverest of ads.

CHAPTER 5

THE COURAGE TO BE DIFFERENT

Competitive strategy is about being different. It means deliberately choosing a different set of activities to deliver a unique mix of value.

—Michael Porter, professor of management
Harvard Business School

If you haven't noticed Chobani yogurt in your grocer's dairy case, you probably will soon. The company has had growth rates in sales, head count, and market capitalization that rival those of Facebook, Google, and others. Chobani is not publicly traded, but it's common knowledge that the company grew annual revenues to $750 million within five years of its founding. It recently eclipsed $1 billion in revenue, a feat reached in approximately ten years. This is the stuff of technology titans like Google and Facebook—not dairy products.[23]

The particularly interesting thing about Chobani's growth is that it was in the face of adversity, naysayers, and doubters. People told Chobani founder Hamdi Ulukaya that his business would never work. He was told that American's wouldn't like the taste of

Greek yogurt, that producing food with natural ingredients wasn't economical, and that owning and operating your own factory was a recipe for disaster. After all, things like that are supposed to be outsourced. These and other tactics employed by Chobani were not just counterintuitive, they were *precisely* why the company took off like a rocket.

When I asked Peter McGuinness, chief marketing and brand officer at Chobani, why the company developed traction before the brand was well known, his answer was simple: "Chobani was different." He elaborated a bit by saying that the company and its products were "pioneering" and unique at a time when the consumer happened to be ready for better choices. Chobani likes to poke fun at mainstream yogurt competitors that include ingredients like "Purple #40" on their product packaging. Chobani is about real ingredients and against artificial flavors and sweeteners.

There are many mundane—perhaps even academic—elements of Formulaic marketing. We can all mostly agree on things like market positioning, mission, and values. But how about courage? The word *courage* isn't found in many marketing textbooks, but it is found in the stories of most successful marketers. The courage to be different, to stand out strategically (not just for the sake of standing out), and to draw a contrast is at the heart of succeeding. If your brand is like that of your competitors, you give buyers no clear reason to choose you over them. Chobani is an example of a company that is not just different, but courageous in its approach in the face of the conventional wisdom and the status quo. Marketing takes guts. And Formulaic marketing blends these courageous differentials, along with the values and stories that drive them, onto a thriving trajectory.

Different Is a Fundamental

Being different isn't just about marketing. Being different is a fundamental to building and positioning a business. Its importance runs deep within an organization, most notably as the cornerstone of business strategy itself. When asked to distill his years of strategic study into simple terms, Harvard Business School professor Michael Porter highlighted the notion of being different as the fundamental concept. "Strategy is about making choices, tradeoffs; it's about deliberately choosing to be different...Strategy 101 is about choices [because] you can't be all things to all people." In other words, you can't be strategic without being different.

We can also look to one of the most iconic ad campaigns of all time for clues to the importance of being different. To accentuate its place in the market, Apple used a campaign slogan for a number of years featuring portraits of iconic minds throughout the years. Names included the likes of Alfred Hitchcock, Charlie Chaplin, Albert Einstein, and Pablo Picasso with two words overlaying their portraits: "think different." The campaign was successful, and the positive emotions it evokes still ripple in society today. Why? Because different is inspirational, transformative, and encouraging.

This doesn't mean that being different is easy. It's difficult, requires risk, and challenges the conventional. As a result, many companies miss this notion altogether and often unknowingly succumb to mediocrity.

Uses Facts Instead of Platitudes to Differentiate

Steve Jobs taught us all to "think different." World-renowned management professor Michael Porter boils the essence of strategic thought to being different. But when it comes to telling your brand's or product's story, be sure to be specific and detailed about how it's different. Establishing your point(s) of differentiation is paramount to competitiveness. But you must root them in facts—not platitudes.

When I hear a commercial for a car company that tells me that "we put quality first" or see a restaurant ad promising that "service matters" to them, I roll my eyes. It makes me think, "Well, I should hope so." I hope that quality is important to a car company and that service matters to a restaurant. I roll my eyes because these platitudes—general statements that are cliché or overused—can be applied to most all companies. But on their own, they're not unique, and they carry little or no weight with today's discerning consumer.

Certainly there's nothing wrong with being committed to quality or service. But brands must be specific when making these claims. Otherwise, the message is washed away with all the others making the same general statements.

As consumers, we're a bit skeptical. When we hear brands tell us something, we don't initially trust them. Growing up, most of were trained to be on the lookout for promises and claims that are too good to be true.

> As consumers, we're a bit skeptical. When we hear brands tell us something, we don't initially trust them. Growing up, most of were trained to be on the lookout for promises and claims that are too good to be true.

Prove to your buyer that these things are important to you by using facts and figures—not platitudes. Don't be lazy. Here are some examples:

- A circuit training program: Instead of saying "the best workout of your life," specify that "most adults over forty can burn twice the calories of a thirty-minute treadmill run."
- A quick-service restaurant: Instead of bragging about "great food at a fair price," tell them that "nine out of ten customers tell us they would come back next week."
- An accounting firm: Instead of proclaiming "client satisfaction," share that "the average tenure of our client relationships is nine years."

- A bed-and-breakfast: Instead of speaking to your "visitor approval," explain that "we have a five-star rating on TripAdvisor."

Alaska Airlines uses its independent rankings (rooted in fact) to prove its commitment to satisfaction. The company was recently ranked as the top airline by the *Wall Street Journal* and J.D. Power—both independent sources—and proudly shares these accolades with stakeholders. Your company, product, or service may very well be an excellent one. Tell us why—but be specific. And if you don't have specifics, go find (or create) a factual, measurable expression of your excellence. In the end, you'll be different.

Being Different Is All Around Us

If you are wondering how to make your business truly different, perhaps it's best to look around you and think about your own behavior. Why do you buy the products you buy? Why do you attend the house of worship you do? Why did you choose the surgeon you did to perform your knee procedure? Our own behaviors signal differences in strategic choices made by brands.

Chobani deliberately chose to include only natural ingredients and to manufacture its own products (as opposed to outsourcing) to control the process end to end, poking fun at competitors whose products include ingredients like "Purple #9." The company has grown like a weed. LaCroix produces carbonated beverages with no sugar, no calories, and no artificial sweeteners, giving consumers a distinct and healthy alternative to soda. With its brightly colored packaging, the company has taken off like a rocket and induced bigger players in the beverage industry to copy it.[24] You can't buy a Coca-Cola at Whole Foods because the supermarket refused to carry any products with high fructose corn syrup, a well-known health risk. Whole Foods is unapologetic about this and publishes a list of "unacceptable" ingredients prominently on its website.[25] The Strand bookstore in Manhattan has much of the same inventory as any Barnes & Noble, but it incorporates rare and used books and only hires people who are avid readers and know about books. The company is thriving in an era in which brick-and-mortar bookstores, especially thriving ones, are as rare as a Hemingway first edition.

A Litmus Test

We all get confused about what truly is different. Having good service at a bed-and-breakfast isn't a true differentiator, any more than deciding to put butter in your bread recipe. Deciding to pursue low-cost suppliers for your products is a sound idea, but in the words of Professor Porter, "That's not a strategy—that's operational effectiveness" or implementing general best practices. These types of things are good to do and have, but they aren't necessarily differentiators in the marketplace.

So how do you know when you have or can create a true difference? A litmus test, a procedure that will help us determine whether something exists or not, is pretty simple. Here is the test: ask yourself whether there is an element of your product or service that is remarkable. The dictionary defines *remarkable* as "worthy of being or likely to be noticed especially as being uncommon or extraordinary," but marketing expert Seth Godin reminds us that the term means simply "Is it worth making a remark [to a friend] about?" In other words, is there something about what you do that is so different that people have to tell others? In his bestselling book, *Contagious: Why Things Catch On*, Wharton School marketing professor Jonah Berger characterizes remarkability as "...what makes something interesting, surprising, or novel."[26]

> Remarkable: worthy of being or likely to be noticed especially as being uncommon or extraordinary.
>
> — Merriam-Webster Dictionary

Remarkable things are all around us, if we look for them. Cirque de Soleil shows, for example, are staggering displays of artistry, acrobatics, risk-taking, talent, and choreography unlike anything else in the world. The Phantom drone produces stunning and incredible images and flight patterns via GPS and stabilization against the elements that are unconventional and mesmerizing. Mattress pioneer Casper sends its mattresses to its customers in surprisingly small boxes through vacuum packaging. The artist David Chihuhly and his works of art on display in places like the Space Needle in Seattle, Washington, and the Bellagio in Las Vegas, Nevada, leave you baffled about how they were conceptualized, let alone created. The hot chocolate in Paris at the Angelina café is world famous for its richness, consistency, and presentation. All these things are not just different; you can't *not* tell someone about them after you experience them. They're remarkable.

Here's why this is highly important. Remarks—not ads—drive purchase decisions, especially in the era of digital marketing and social media. David Edelman, coleader of McKinsey & Company's Global Digital Marketing Strategy practice makes this crystal clear in a foundational *Harvard Business Review* article. Though his research, he found that, while up to 90 percent of marketing dollars go to woo new consumers in the consideration stage of buying, the "single most powerful impetus to buy is often someone else's advocacy."[27] Positive word of mouth moves the sales needle, and that only comes from delivering an outstanding product or service.

These differentiators don't always have to be monumental or world famous (although that is nice); they can simply be differences in features or attributes that draw a contrast. Amazon's video-streaming service, the chief competitor of which is Netflix, is a good example of this. While both services feature a different (yet fairly similar) variety of recorded movies and television shows that you can stream while your television, tablet, or device is connected to the Internet, Amazon's service features a key (perhaps temporary) difference. Through licensing arrangements and/or technology, Amazon's service allows users to actually download and view content off-line, something Netflix does not offer. The David versus Goliath battle of 16,000 Movies against Blockbuster Video is also a good example of how small differences can drive competitiveness. 16,000 Movies gave away free popcorn to customers and also allowed them to reserve VHS tapes, neither of which was offered by Blockbuster. Both the Amazon and 16,000 Movies examples illustrate how small differences in product offerings can create meaningful distinctions for consumers that are worth talking about. In other words, they're remarkable.

Simple Ways to Differentiate

Unlike the team at Cirque de Soleil, we don't have to risk our lives to be remarkable. There are all sorts of ways to develop differentiators, large or small.

Delta Airlines gets travelers from one city to the next every day, just like any other airline. But it does many things differently throughout the travel process that make me prefer the airline and seek to travel on it whenever I have a choice, often willing to pay a little more to do so. Delta has a really powerful mobile app, excellent technology at gates and in terminals, and a palpable commitment to customer satisfaction. During a recent, slight delay at a Delta gate due to the illness of a crew member, the staff brought out free snacks and bottled water for those waiting for the flight. It was a small gesture that made a big difference.

You have to think long and hard about how to differentiate, though. Imitating someone else in order to appear different isn't being original at all. That's copying. Ritz-Carlton made saying "my pleasure" to customers famous, and then others ran to imitate. It reminds me of the classic scene in the film *There's Something About Mary* when Ben Stiller picks up a hitchhiker whose business "idea" is to create a workout video called *7-Minute Abs* to combat the popular *8-Minute Abs.* It's missing the point. Don't copy, and don't differentiate in ways that are easily copied.

Doubletree Hotels gives you free cookies at check-in. I once worked with a legal mediation firm that baked fresh bread in the office to create a more homey atmosphere. Olive Garden gives customers Andes mints with the check, which have become a fun expectation at the end of a meal. Patagonia takes new sign-ups to its catalog on the telephone, rather than through an electronic form on its website, with a live operator who works for Patagonia, instead of a third-party call center somewhere offshore. If you call them, you'll notice how they sound like a true part of California culture, going so far as to offer you free stickers by mail. These examples prove that you don't have to do much to make a huge difference in your customers' experience. Here are some simple questions to get you started:

- Can we create or define a methodology that represents a different way of doing what we do, building what we build, or making what we make?
- Can we do some research and/or create intellectual property that gives us a distinctive advantage over others?
- Can we create a feature of our product that no one else has?
- Can we make our promotional materials truly different and distinguishable when compared to those of our competitors?
- Can we specifically serve an identifiable market segment in a different way than has ever been done before?
- Might we identify some area of our business that we can truly be the best in the world at?
- Can we earn specific accreditation or licensure that others can't?
- Can we create, develop, or acquire something proprietary?
- What can we do that has never been done before?

Being different is a required component of a Formulaic approach to marketing. You must find a way to stand out in order to be noticed and to resonate with someone who understands that difference, appreciates it, and will go out of his or her way to experience it, time and again. Standing out is now without risk, clearly, but it can be nurtured and cultivated with courage to a point at which it becomes a badge of honor. Like the "Keep Austin Weird" mantra of Austin, Texas, being different can quickly go from being risky to being cool, with the right amount of conviction and backbone. So figure out how you *are* different, *be* different, and be unapologetic about the differences.

CHAPTER 6

AN INTIMATE KNOWLEDGE OF WHO YOU EXIST TO SERVE

> Don't market to the middle. The middle is boring. The middle is lame.
>
> —Peter McGuinness, chief marketing officer
> Chobani Yogurt

It's been said that if you try to be all things to all people, you'll end up being nothing to no one. And marketers can be the worst. We tend to characterize success by sheer volume and by big numbers: page views, customers, subscribers, and sales. And with good reason. Our culture tells us that big is good and that big equals success.

But an inadvertent focus on volume tends to water down product offerings. In an effort to appeal to everyone, brands don't really thrill anyone. You see it when a sandwich shop starts selling sushi on the side or when a brand that makes athletic gear starts a line of business casual clothing. The sushi ends up being mediocre at best, and consumers end up falling out of love with the athletic gear because the business casual clothing misses the mark.

I agree with Peter McGuinness, CMO of Chobani, when during a recent keynote address, he implored the audience of marketers to not "market to the middle." The middle, he said, is boring, lame, and where brands go to die. Chobani has done the opposite, he explained, in focusing on a small market segment with a common set of ideals and values and building relationships with them. Chobani ended up driving volume in the end, but only after satisfying a small market segment extremely well with a superior product and alternative approach.

Avoiding the middle has been the key ingredient to success for a number of brands. Starting small doesn't mean that volume won't come later. Quite the opposite, in fact. Satisfying a narrow group of customers with a superior product results in a fan base that talks and talks and talks about your product. Many brands that ultimately get big, thriving and growing in wide markets, got there by starting small.

The lesson for all of us is to focus long and hard on a small segment first and on making them raving fans. Even though you start small, you just might end up with a world-class product or brand. Most importantly, you'll become something to someone. Formulaic marketers focus on narrow markets—very defined segments of buyers—and commit relentlessly to pleasing them.

Identifying Your Someone

There's an old agency joke that pokes fun at the client longing to sell product to everyone who is willing to pay for it. It quotes the typical client as saying "our target audience is males and females age zero and up." In reality, this attitude shows a lack of focus and represents a serious problem in the business.

> Our target audience is males and females aged zero and up.

Who is it that you really exist to serve? Who, to the tee, has specific needs, wants, whims, desires, aspirations, or longings that your product or service meets? Many marketers are reluctant to narrow the audience for their products because they fear eliminating.

Consider YETI, a brand of high-priced coolers, tumblers, and associated gear that helps people (almost magically) keep ice frozen for days on end or a cup of coffee hot during an eight-hour drive. If you walk into most big-box sporting goods or camping stores like Dick's Sporting Goods or REI, you'll see displays of the product for the mainstream consumer. YETI has become popular among the masses in less than a ten-year period, with annual sales in the neighborhood of one billion dollars.

But it wasn't always that way. Cofounders (and brothers) Ryan Seiders and Roy Seiders didn't start out contemplating how to sell a cooler to every single person who needed to buy one. Instead, they focused on solving the specific problems they had while hunting and fishing, assuming others faced the same ones. They knew that they needed a cooler that would be extremely durable during travel, in the elements, and in potentially extreme conditions. They needed one that was highly durable when being tossed around a boat or moving vehicle—one that could even double as a platform that an angler could stand on while fishing.[28]

They set out to build a super durable (and expensive, by the way) cooler that lived up to promises and became a word-of-mouth sensation among serious hunters, campers, and fishermen. They engaged brand ambassadors indigenous to those communities, including "influential guides and fishermen" (according to an *Inc.* magazine profile), instead of marketing to the average soccer mom, toting orange slices to the field for a halftime snack. The results speak for themselves—rocketing sales, brand strength, and an ultimate presence in the mainstream. The rest of us caught up only later.

Your brand needs a *someone*. Perhaps it needs more than one someone. Some brands focus on a few different segments. But thriving brands are focused on specific audience segments, and not just to avoid being the punch line of that old agency joke.

Paint a Picture of Your Audience Member

Once you decide who you want to serve, it is helpful to develop a profile of the person. It helps to narrow your focus with respect to the product, its features, the language and expressions to use when communicating with that segment, and even imagery and color selections. And just like your mission, values, and cultural blueprint, it's important to document who your audience segments are for the sake of clarity and institutionalization. The portrait of who you serve should become a part of your brand.

Lululemon, the revered maker of athletic leisure apparel, exemplifies this quite well. The company created a profile of a fictional audience member called Ocean, "a 32-year-old professional single woman who makes $100,000 a year…she's engaged, has her own condo, is traveling, fashionable, and has an hour and a half to work out a day" and another, a male named Duke, "an athletic opportunist who enjoys surfing in the summer and snowboarding in the winter."[29] Lululemon refers to their audience profiles as "muses" and uses them internally to contemplate company strategy, product development, and company communications. Employees are well acquainted with both Ocean and Duke and look to them as a collective focal point for company direction.

We can learn from the Lululemon illustration how developing profiles of audience members helps to get a picture of exactly who you're trying to satisfy. The more you know about them, the better you will be able to serve them. As you contemplate who your audience segments are, here are a few things to consider in profiling them:

- What are their names? Giving them names helps you humanize the profiles and gives you a common frame of reference within the team. Get creative. Our agency recently profiled a segment for a client and named her "Aspiring

Annie," to remind us all that she is a young professional climbing the corporate ladder.

- What are their demographic attributes? It is important to profile age, gender, income, and other demographic details to help understand generational issues, lifestyle tendencies, and levels of disposable income.
- What are their hobbies? Knowing what someone does with his or her free time helps us to understand how he or she lives, what choices he or she is likely to make, and how he or she relaxes.
- What are their preferences in terms of entertainment, brands, and food? A Taco Bell addict who binges on smart Netflix television shows is different from someone who avoids gluten and doesn't own a television. Painting a picture of someone's lifestyle choices helps us understand how to reach him or her.
- What else might we imagine about them? There is no single right answer in terms of profiling an audience segment. It's just important that you get creative in any way that you see fit in terms of painting a picture of it. Feel free to talk about where they live, where they go on vacation, and how they take their coffee. Be creative, and be real.
- What do they look like? Associate photographs or sketches of them. What they wear, what kind of physical shape they are in, and even their hairstyles tell us something about them.

You can often reference the relationships among different audience segments. Sometimes it is sensible to assume that one audience segment might influence another. In a recent client exercise for a new consumer product, we determined that our primary audience segment, a mother of two, would have a high degree of influence on her husband's decision to try the product. We also determined that that the mother would be initially influenced by her younger, single friend, who she typically looks to for fashion and lifestyle trends and ideas.

Once developed, audience profiles can be leveraged in many ways. For starters, they give you and your marketing teammates a frame of reference for the type of language and communication styles to use. What should our logo or name for a product look like? What types of colors would be most resonant? What social media channels will be most appropriate? What types of content are most likely to be consumed, engaged with, and liked? All these choices can be looked at through the lens of the audience profiles. So contemplate them, wrestle with their nuances, and then document and circulate them to your team. Audience profiles will guide you through a myriad of challenging decisions and simplify and clarify many of them for you along the way.

If nothing else, develop a simple written sketch of who you aspire to serve and please. A successful, emerging restaurant group called Hawkers, an Asian street fare concept based in Florida, defines its audience very briefly yet succinctly: "our customer is a foodie, culturally affluent, savvy with social media, and can point out Asia on a map."

> Our customer is a foodie, culturally affluent, savvy with social media, and can point out Asia on a map.
>
> — Kaleb Harrell
> Co-Founder, Hawkers

That one descriptor, albeit brief, helps Hawkers with the rest of what I would characterize as its Formulaic marketing pursuits. It can guide everything from the colors it chooses in its promotional materials to the language the social media team uses to update its customers on Facebook.

Understanding Expectations

If you are my customer, how do I know how to meet your expectations if I don't even know what they are? I can make assumptions, certainly, but the burden is on me to go one step further and actually find out. Knowing and understanding (if not anticipating) the expectations of my customers is critical with respect to serving them well.

> If you are my customer, how do I know how to meet your expectations if I don't even know what they are? I can make assumptions, certainly, but the burden is on me to go one step further and actually find out.

A major part of pleasing your specific market segments is in understanding what they need and expect in the first place. The Subway restaurant in the Houston airport knows full well that their passengers don't have much time to waste—they expect their sandwiches to be prepared quickly. Chobani customers expect that anything with the Chobani brand name on it will be healthy. Formulaic marketers know how to meet and exceed expectations because they take the time to learn what they are.

The Left Behind

Choosing your audience segments and narrowing in on them means that you have to leave some people behind. Getting back to the notion of "you can't be all things to all people," there is often a temptation to stay broad so we don't leave anyone behind. But as a marketer who wants to succeed, you must leave some, if not most, behind. Not everyone will be able to afford the forty-five-dollar entrée, and some will not be influenced by the fact that your ingredients are all natural. But marketers are often reluctant to let go of any audience segment because they want to reserve the right to sell one of their widgets to anyone.

It will seem unfathomable to leave someone, if not most people, behind, but if you aren't excluding the masses from your marketing focus. But as a marketer, you can relax. Just because you profile three audience segments and not the hundreds of others at your disposal doesn't mean you can't ultimately sell them one of your widgets—it just means that you're specifically positioned for just a few. Narrowing your focus is an early step toward thriving.

The contrast between Dunkin Donuts and Starbucks is a good one to consider in this regard. If you walk into a Starbucks, you'll notice warm lighting, trendy music, plenty of comfortable places to sit and work, free Internet connectivity. Starbucks aspires to be your "third place"—a third location in your life, beyond your home and place of business, where you can work, study, meet with friends, or just hang out. Dunkin Donuts, on the other hand, takes the opposite approach. Lights are bright, furniture is less than comfortable, and there's no musical program to speak of.

But Dunkin takes that approach for a reason. "We're not the place for you if you want to spend four hours working on a screenplay or looking for your next job," says chief marketing officer John Costello. Dunkin positions itself as the destination for the everyday American who is hard at work and on the go. It's very recognizable slogan, "American Runs on Dunkin," has also become its statement of purpose. Its product experience is for "everyday folks who keep American running, keep themselves running every day" according to Costello. Dunkin has succeeded by not feeling like it also has to cater to the eclectic, intercontinental preferences of would-be Starbucks customers, who might prefer a product and/or experience offering that is more nuanced. Both have succeeded by focusing on their target audiences through a particular lens and accepting that some will be left behind. That said, people from both camps likely buy coffee from both at times. There's no law against it!

> We're not the place for you if you want to spend the next four hours working on a screen-play or looking for your next job.
>
> — John Costello
> Chief Marketing Officer, Dunkin Donuts

So once you figure out who you want to serve and who you might leave behind, many other things come into focus. Knowing who your customer truly is helps you understand what you should start doing and what you might stop doing in the process. And the more you end up learning about the customer on whom you are placing laser focus, the more the floodgates of creative thought will open with respect to new products to develop, different events to host, new avenues of research to pursue, and fertile areas of intellectual property to cultivate. In the end, you will be free to fully please one specific person or group of persons and relieved of the burden of pleasing everyone. Formulaic marketers don't try to please everyone—just the few segments to whom they are committed.

CHAPTER 7

SOMETHING FITTING TO SELL

It's about the product, not the marketing.

—Bobbi Brown, chief creative officer
Bobbi Brown Cosmetics

One of our agency's long-term clients is MVP Sports, a group of health and fitness clubs across the country that stands for excellence, customer service, and community engagement. As I was walking through one of the locations recently, I saw the office of a personal trainer with a poster prominently displayed. The poster was of an alluring cupcake, with the following caption: "No workout program can fix a bad diet." This was a very ironic and eye-catching image that I certainly haven't forgotten, but it made me think of the following parallel in marketing: "No promotional program can fix a bad product."

No promotional program can fix a bad product.

It's critical to know who you are, what you stand for, and how you're different—and to write it down. But one of the major drivers of brand success is the association with a product that is not just adequate or suitable, but awesome. In the four *P*s of marketing— product, price, place, and promotion—product is first for a reason.

To follow a hunch and prove a point, I recently threw out a question to my Facebook friends. I simply asked my local friends what their favorite restaurant in the area was and why. Of the dozen or so answers I received, I got six different restaurant names. (Some agreed on their favorite, with some superstars getting more than one vote.) My friends went on to cite things like food, atmosphere, service, and location as rationales for the selections. None mentioned the brilliance of the advertising campaign as the reason! Actually, of the six, I noted that none of them are prominent advertisers—you don't see them on billboards or in television ads and barely even on social media. Hawkers, the aforementioned Asian street fare restaurant concept, has achieved all its growth with little or no advertising—only word-of-mouth promotion online and off-line. To illustrate the point even further, consider the thriving pizza restaurant in Las Vegas adjacent to The Cosmopolitan hotel. It has rave reviews on social media and is packed with repeat customers but has no sign, no visibility and not even a name. Customers have nicknamed it "Secret Pizza."

While I'm not advising companies not to advertise, I am firm on a point: a truly remarkable product experience finds a way to promote itself. The product is the marketing, not the promotion. And Formulaic marketers thrive in large part because the product that they have to sell is not only worth making a remark about, but also particularly pleasing to the audience segments that they know and understand so intimately. It simply fits.

Marketing Is More Than Just Promotion

When revenue is disappointing, marketers and small-business owners grapple with what to do with their marketing efforts. I often hear remarks like "We're struggling with how to market ourselves" or "We need some new marketing ideas." When I listen, I often detect a subtle nuance that reveals that an expanded view of marketing would be helpful.

What the person is really trying to say is "We're struggling with how to promote ourselves" or "We need some new promotional ideas." They've limited their view of what marketing is. Marketing is more than just promotion. Classical marketing theory teaches us that there are four *P*s within the marketing function: product (or service), price, place (or distribution channel), and promotion.[30] This collection is often referred to as the marketing mix or the four *P*s of marketing. My first college marketing professor defined marketing in this way: "Marketing is the practice of satisfying the customer at a profit involving a total company effort." Note that this definition says nothing about advertising, public relations, or sales promotion.

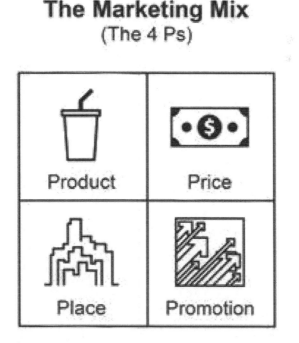

The Marketing Mix
(The 4 Ps)

Product	Price
Place	Promotion

Marketing is much more than just promotion as demonstrated in the diagram above.

Following this thinking, if a business is not thriving from a revenue perspective, it may very well be that the issue has nothing to do with promotional tactics (i.e., advertising, public relations, web presence etc.). It may very well have to do with one of the other three *P*s. Here are some common ailments that I see:

- A company's product (or service) is not really attractive to people, and it needs an adjustment or a replacement. It may need some new feature or component to make it more attractive.
- The price is too high. The price of the product or service may be too high compared to those of your competitors. You might need a price adjustment.
- The price is too low. When comparing your product to others, customers may perceive that yours is of lower quality. They may assume that you get what you pay for and be turned off. "After all," people think, "how can anything worthwhile be so cheap?"
- Your place (or location or distribution channel) is not great. You might have a good product, but it's not in a place where enough people are or have easy access to. Brick-and-mortar sellers might consider other physical locations, while online sellers might look at markets like Amazon.com or eBay to reach new buyers.

These are just a few of the issues you might want to remedy. The important thing is to look at marketing from a thirty-thousand-foot perspective and consider its many facets. Your promotion may very well be just right and will perform beautifully if you fix something else.

Taking a Broader View of Product

For the purposes of this book, it's important for us to develop a framework for thinking about the word *product*. After all, what is a product? Most people assume that a product is a tangible item that you can see, touch, or hold in your hand: the physical manifestation of manufacturing and/or assembly. Most of us think about products as things like razor blades, a set of reading glasses, a sports car, or a screwdriver.

But what about Stanley Steemer, the carpet cleaning company? That brand doesn't really deliver anything tangible, except clean carpets. They perform a service. For all intents and purposes, the same goes for law firms, accounting firms, and advertising agencies. As such, we must broaden our definition of *product* to encompass the delivery of a service. If your brand is service-oriented (which may very well be the case, as our economy has shifted from a product economy to a service economy), then your service *is* your product.

Also critical to the delivery of either a product or a service is the way in which it is delivered. Did the representative of the company make you, as a customer, feel valued and appreciated? Was it delivered on time? Did it meet your expectations? Did the company bother to learn about your expectations?

Apart from the way in which the product or service was delivered, we can't ignore its quality. Was it sturdy and durable? If it was food, was it pleasing to you in terms of taste, temperature, freshness, and consistency? If the product was the rental of a hotel room, was it clean, functional, and comfortable?

Bobbi Brown, chief creative officer of Bobbi Brown cosmetics, is firm on this point. She credits product—not promotion—as the defining factor in successful marketing, something that runs contrary to popular thinking. Her product line took off when she saw a void in the merchandise counter for "a lipstick that looked like lips, only better" and an admonition that "the secret to beauty is simple: be who you are."[31] Her products can now be found in some of the most prestigious department stores in the world.

A big element of the product is the presence of trappings and features. My father, a management professor, has written and published more than sixty-five college textbooks over the course of more than forty years. Over that time, I watched him spend hour upon hour composing paragraphs and chapters that turned into books. Regardless of the quality of all the text that he painstakingly composed, he told me how surprised he always was that the buyers of this products (the professors) often seemed to be less focused on the content of the books themselves and more interested in what came along with the books: the study guides, professor notes, accompanying videos, and the like. In essence, features of the product were important to the buyer than the core products themselves.

Another important dimension of the product is how it is packaged. What does the box, bag, or container say about the product? Apple products are placed within boxes that are crafted, fitted, and conceived with tremendous detail. Apple doesn't just put products in boxes and call it a day. It goes to the moon and back to make the package a part of the experience.

People upload, share, and watch videos of "unboxing" products to show the experience of unpackaging a product and "meeting" it for the first time. Nathan Clark, founder of Wondermade, a crafter of gourmet marshmallows, said he put great effort into his product packaging to make it "beautiful" and "fun to hold" in an interview. Instead of just throwing the marshmallows in a premade cardboard box, he sourced his own materials and hired a throwback letterpress printer.[32] If you contrast this with the inexpensive plastic bag that marshmallows typically come in, it's easy to see how value is conveyed before the package is even opened. Study after study tells us that packaging influences consumer perception. The package is part of the product.

For these reasons and more, Formulaic marketers take a broad view of what a product actually is. To frame this view, it is helpful to define a product as the sum total of value, benefit, and feeling received by the customer in exchange for its price. A product isn't just a widget—it's an experience.

Focus on Product Excellence

Our agency is in Orlando, and we work in and around tourism quite a bit. A reporter doing a piece on tourism marketing called and asked me the following question: What is the best thing that a tourist-related business can do to attract more visitors and customers?

I'm pretty sure he was looking for a silver bullet or a secret weapon that all hotels, theme parks, and restaurants could employ. He was fishing for a traditional promotional tip like

- buy a Facebook ad,
- print brochures and put them in visitor centers on Orlando highways, and
- optimize your web page for keywords like *best Orlando hotels* and *great Orlando restaurants.*

While none of these ideas is bad, they're very different from a core, transcendent thought that I believe is, indeed, a silver bullet. My answer? Tell the restaurant or tourist attraction to provide a remarkable experience. I think he was disappointed. After all, this isn't a gimmick or an ointment that can be applied to the problem of a low-traffic restaurant.

But here's why I answered that way: the reason this is important is that a remarkable experience (read: an experience worth making a remark about) is one that carries the day in marketing. It's the most valuable currency in today's consumer world of not enough time and too many choices.

Consumers start their trips months before they leave, on places like TripAdvisor, Yelp, and Facebook. They ask their friends who have been to Orlando on Facebook where they should visit when they get there. They seek reviews on TripAdvisor from people they have never met. In short, they trust their peers, not what you print on a brochure. And if you're not creating a remarkable experience for your guests, you're not a part of their remarks. It's just that simple.

To be remarkable, you have to be bold and unique. You have to have guts, and you have to care. Here are a couple of ideas, and not just for tourism-related businesses:

- If you're a chef, come out and greet your guests, and ask them how they enjoyed the food. Really ask and really care. Bring them a dessert sample that they didn't ask for.
- If you're a hotel, give your guests warm cookies when they check in.
- When guests leave, offer them a free bottle of water for the road.
- Learn your guests' names, and ask them to come back soon. Remember and acknowledge them when they come back. If they have a special preference, make a note of it.
- Design your space and location to be interesting, fun, clean, and inspiring.
- Exude enthusiasm and gratitude for the presence of the customer in front of you.

Every business has more than one way to enhance its operation and make it unique. The more you put into it, the more remarkable you will be…and the fewer gimmicks you will seek.

Setting Expectations

Whether you like it or not, your product or experience will come with expectations. I alluded to this in the previous chapter with regard to intimately understanding your audience. And do you know how we define disappointment? It's when expectations are not met. So it's important that a product experience is consistent with regard to how it delivers on expectations. Whether consumers know it or not, they carry them around and will judge you based upon how your product delivers.

When I go to your restaurant, will the experience be super speedy, slow and lingering, or somewhere in between? Customers should know and count on the answers, so they know where to go when they are in a rush and where to celebrate a special occasion with a loved one. Will those running shoes stand up to pretty heavy wear and tear, or should I spend thirty bucks more to get the more durable pair? Lifelong runners will want to know what to count on, so they'll buy your products for decades to come. Will your portable speaker be durable enough to stand up to monthly trips to the beach, or will it be weak when it encounters a few grains of sand? Let me know, because I will make future decisions to buy other, related products like surround-sound systems, outdoor speakers, and headphones based on my experiences. In most instances, I'll tell my friends.

Expectations can be set low because we don't always want or need the best of the best. A cheap pair of sunglasses is a cheap pair of sunglasses; I don't need anything special when I forget to pack mine for vacation. The same goes for a cheap pair of flip-flops or a portable cell phone car charger for the rental car trip I didn't know I was going to have to take. Don't promise premium when all I need is regular.

But the main idea for marketers is not to disappoint the customer by not only meeting expectations, but also exceeding them. Leading theme parks get this one right. It is rumored by experts that when they post signs near long lines that say "your wait time from this point is approximately twenty minutes," the actual time is a few minutes less, erring on the side of underpromising or portraying a worst-case scenario. Whether you are waiting in line to go on a roller coaster or for a table in a themed restaurant, the calculations on the sign are designed to leave you feeling pleasantly surprised instead of disappointed throughout your day in the park. As a brand, you can set the expectations and seek to overdeliver on your underpromise.

We're Not for Everyone, and That's OK

In the 1960s, an eleven-year-old boy became interested in golf and golf equipment. His love for the game turned into a passion for design and construction of golf clubs—specifically, putters. He started designing and fashioning putters in the garage of his California home. He developed a passion for the look, feel, weight, balance, and performance of putters. His passion extended to the sound the putter made when it made contact with the ball, the design of the cover that protected it from harm during travel, and of course its ability to help a player roll the ball into the golf hole.

Decades later, Scott "Scotty" Cameron is known as a "rock star" of golf, helping player after player win amateur games and major championships. In a recent stretch of forty major men's golf championships, Cameron's putters were used by fifteen of the winners. His products have helped player after player win tournaments like the Masters and the US Open, including the likes of Tiger Woods and Jordan Spieth.

The putters, with unique names like Futura, Newport and My Girl, are also thought of as collectibles by amateur golfers around the world. ZZ Top drummer Frank Beard has a collection of Scotty Cameron putters valued at nearly $1.5 million. They feature options for customizations like monogramming, icons, and his famous red alignment dots. His passion for his products is palpable: "Naysayers said that we [don't] need another putter maker, so I tried to be the best putter maker."[33]

Cameron's company has gone from zero dollars in sales when it started to over one hundred million dollars annually. He commands nearly four hundred dollars for most of his putters, while competitors are only able to command between 25 and 50 percent of that. Due to his pricing, his putters aren't for everyone—in fact, they're for a small fraction of the golfing market. Other club manufacturers sell an entire set of clubs for less than that. Cameron's recipe for success is to create an excellent product that caters specifically to a particular audience. And it is clearly working.

Naysayers said that we [don't] need another putter maker, so I tried to be the best putter maker.

— Scotty Cameron
Founder, Scotty Cameron

The Cameron example shows us how a particular product fits a particular audience segment and not the rest. The message? Our product is not for everyone, and that's OK.

The Dunkin Donuts and Starbucks contrast is also helpful here. The Dunkin product experience and brand promise is specifically and unapologetically designed for the person who has little time to sit and enjoy the experience, while Starbucks is quite the opposite. As I alluded to before with respect to serving a narrow market segment and excluding others, those who try to please all people with a product experience will be hamstrung.

Being Formulaic requires that what you sell—your product, your service, and/or the experience you deliver—fits your narrow audience segment like a glove. If your product isn't remarkable in such a way that it strikes a chord with your audience segment, then the segment will not go out of its way to pay you for the product in the future, let alone make a remark about it to others.

CHAPTER 8

A COMMITMENT TO BECOME A BRAND PUBLISHER

> Content is really the only marketing that's left.
>
> —Seth Godin

There used to be only three channels on television. There used to be printed newspapers on most every doorstep in every home and every office—in some cases, both a morning and an evening edition. People used to walk to the mailbox, waiting for a printed edition of *Sports Illustrated*, *Newsweek*, or *Time* to show up. Consumers used to watch commercials. Readers used to comb through classified ads and call people on the telephone to make deals.

In that environment, corporations behaved differently in order to gain exposure for their products and services. They used to create advertisements for television shows that consumers would watch. They also used to create and place display ads in newspapers that people would actually read and take out full-page ads in magazines that dominated coffee tables. They would also call reporters and submit press releases in the mail or via facsimile, which would be reprinted in newspapers by dedicated columnists.

As these circumstances have changed completely, the game has changed dramatically as well. The media landscape is completely different. There are still commercials on television, but we usually fast-forward through them using our DVRs. Magazines are still printed, but circulations are on the floor, and many longtime stalwarts don't print them anymore. Most print columnists no longer have full-time jobs with major media outlets but instead have launched or participate in online ventures, where their work is circulated digitally. Anxious to find new streams of revenue to replace evaporating ad sales, publishers like *New York Times* have begun to act as ad agencies in terms of creating branded content for clients.[34] There are several hundred television channels and networks now. Instead of walking to their doorsteps to pick up the newspaper, consumers launch Facebook and Twitter to get their news. If there is a major news story happening, they can open Twitter on the Wi-Fi-enabled airplane instead of waiting to land to find a television. If they face a problem, they go to Google more often than calling a friend and asking for the answer. Whether consumers are experiencing medical symptoms or are trying to fix an ice maker, Google is easier, faster, and cheaper than calling a friend or family member—let alone going to Home Depot and bothering an employee.

In this changing landscape, the answer for corporations is to change as well. The behavior of their customers has changed, and theirs should too. The corporate marketer is going to be severely disappointed (and probably without a job) if he or she sends a press release to a reporter via fax or uses the whole advertising budget to place a thirty-second commercial during a broadcast of *The Bachelor*, which will be fast-forwarded through by the whole audience.

So how should the behavior of the marketer change in this environment? Quite simply, marketers must create, publish, and promote high-quality content of their own making as a way of thriving within the changing landscape of media consumption. Corporations must face the notion that it is now part of their duty to market through content they actually create instead of latching onto content created by others. Formulaic marketers understand this and embrace the shift in the media landscape.

What Is Content Marketing?

Content marketing has many definitions. Broadly speaking, content marketing is a strategic approach to the changing media consumption landscape. Tactically speaking, I define content marketing as the creation and distribution of content that informs and influences a particular audience but does not advertise or sell.[35]

Even though *content marketing* is a newer term, it's been around for centuries. You can see it in the early 1900s, when John Deere began publishing a magazine for family farms, and in the 1950s, when Jell-O started going door to door with free recipe books that called for the product. You can see it in the same time period, when Proctor & Gamble started producing—literally hiring the actors, writers, and producers—and broadcasting daytime romance serial dramas for their buyers, which ultimately became known as soap operas.

The difference now is that any brand marketer (not just global brand names) can participate. The barriers to entry for starting a blog, an e-mail newsletter, a YouTube channel, or a Facebook page are minimal. The tools are there; the barriers are not. But what is often missing is the creativity, discipline, and initiative for marketers to embrace content marketing and become brand publishers.

Start Thinking of Yourself as a Publisher

As a consumer, are you sick of ads? Do they annoy you? If you're like most of us, advertisements are an invasion, an intrusion, and an interruption. That's why most of us install pop-up blockers and fast-forward through television commercials. As a society, we don't generally like ads.

Just think about your online reading habits. Have you ever been trying to read an article online when an ad pops up, and you're forced to find the "click to close" box just to get to the information you want? It's super annoying and frustrating—especially on your mobile phone. It can take me two or three attempts to properly find the *x* with my finger. It's not helpful to the brand trying to advertise; it's harmful.

So what's a brand to do? After all, advertising is an articulation that you want to reach the consumer and build a relationship. My answer? Instead of being the ad, become the article. Your brand has the opportunity to ditch the ad and become the content.

So how do you do this? For starters, think about what elements of your brand connect with your customers and the things that might inform, educate, inspire, motivate, or touch them. Here are a couple of examples:

- An athletic apparel company might produce an e-mail newsletter containing fitness tips and motivational quotes.
- A car company can create a printed magazine on engineering or craftsmanship.
- A consulting firm might produce a printed journal containing articles on best practices for executives and managers.
- A health food store should start a blog on nutrition.

Examples of content marketing or inbound marketing are all around us. As consumers find ways to move away from ads, marketers are following suit. After all, being the article instead of the ad is an opportunity to be a positive, helpful part of the consumer's life, instead of something that's merely in the way.

Patagonia has put content creation at the center of its marketing effort. The company has a book division called Patagonia Books, which produces films on topics like the environment, climbing, and conservation, and regularly publishes stories on its website and social media channels. The primary goal of its catalog—which traditionally is about selling products for most companies—is "to share and encourage a particular philosophy of life."

How Content Becomes the Answer

If you've made the commitment to become a brand publisher and begin creating content, you start to see things work in ways in which you never imagined. If you truly have dug into your audience segments, developed profiles for the people you wish to serve, and know the things they care about, you're on your way. If you published a series of questions and answers on your company blog that deal with problems your customers face, they'll start showing up in Google searches. After all, Google values original content that contains useful information for users. In public statement after public statement, Google points webmasters to the creation of content—not the jamming of keywords onto web pages—as a primary method to climb in results.[36]

In addition to favorable search results, you will begin to see increases in social media engagement on channels like Facebook, LinkedIn, and Twitter. Since you've taken the time to understand your audience segments and know them so well, you'll have a good idea of what their social media behavior is like—specifically, which channels they use most often. If the content truly resonates with them—either through being entertaining, inspiring, helpful, useful, funny, or emotive—they'll want to pass it along to their friends online. Think about when you've done this in the past. It's likely been for one of those reasons—not because it's an ad for a company. It's good reason to remember to create content that is not self-serving to the brand, but interesting to the audience.

You'll also be in a good position to gain the attention of other blogs, journalists, and online publications. General Mills, maker of cereals like Wheaties, Cheerios, and Golden Grahams, has seen this happen in its blog entitled *The Taste of General Mills*. General Mills uses the blog "to tell the stories [they] want to tell." Over time, the blog has "[given] journalists a reason to pick up the phone and call." Its blog posts have helped it land placements in national media publications like NPR, *Fortune*, NBC News, and *The New York Times*.[37]

When your content resonates with people, they'll forward it to others, and you'll see growth in social media. If it's funny or interesting, Instagram users will tag their friends in the posts, so they'll be notified that there's something to see. New viewers become new followers. Your e-mail subscriber list will grow because the content you create will be so fitting to the audience that they'll share it with their friends, and their friends will become subscribers as well. The research you've done will also attract links from other blogs. These inbound links will signal to Google that your information just received a "vote," and your rankings will improve. The snowball will continue to grow as it rolls down the hill!

No Fear

When I speak to some marketers or business owners about the idea of giving away information and not charging for it, many of them become skittish. An attorney might say "Why would I give away content for free to people instead of charging them for it?" The thinking is sound. After all, if an attorney is paid to dispense advice, why would he or she want to post it for free on a website and negate the need for a phone call, consultation, or case? That said, this fear is irrational.

A person who needs to hire an attorney for a real estate transaction, estate plan, or civil suit can rarely get all he or she needs from a blog post. Potential clients will still need to engage a certified professional to handle filings or represent them in front of a judge or opposing party. The blog post it just the gateway to the transaction between client and professional—not the be-all and end-all.

The music industry has dealt with this issue since the Internet came along and the distribution of pirated content became so pervasive. Over time, artists and publishers have had to come to grips with the fact that that their music will be pirated and posted on publicly available sites like YouTube. The problem has become too big to contain or deal with. Smart artists and publishers have looked for ways to ride the wave instead of fighting it. Award-winning recording artist and Rock and Roll Hall of Fame member John (Cougar) Mellencamp looks at his recorded music as his "gateway" to other streams of revenue. When asked about piracy and the community's not paying for music, Mellencamp explained it this way: "My music is just my calling card now," implying that leveraging the spread of his music online to drive ticket revenue, merchandise sales, and special appearances is the new model for success.[38]

> My music is just my calling card now.
>
> — John (Cougar) Mellencamp

Consider, also, an interesting example from Geek Squad, the company that installs and fixes computers, televisions, and other electronic devices for consumers. The company is a big believer in providing free instructional videos to consumers online. Ironically, these videos explain how to solve problems that the company normally charges for. Doesn't this undermine the company's revenue? According to Robert Stephens, Geek Squad founder, the opposite actually occurs: "Our best customers are the people that think they can fix it themselves," he explains.[39] Presumably, informative and influential content brings users closer to the brand—not further away. And then they buy.

This shift in mind-set from fear to opportunity—from relying on old-line media to embracing today's digital media ecosystem—is common to thriving brands. Their Formulaic approach to marketing places content at the heart of connecting with the customers they have come to know so well. Thriving companies also tell stories through content as a means of connecting with known market segments. In this way, content can be used to educate, to entertain, and to ingratiate. Simply put, thriving brands publish. And the content they create is an essential element of Formulaic marketing.

CHAPTER 9

A BALANCED PROMOTIONAL ATTACK

> Advertising is the price you pay for unremarkable thinking.
>
> —Jeff Bezos, founder and CEO
> Amazon

One of the major premises of this book is that promotion without a firm foundation can yield frustration, wasted money, and disenchantment with marketing altogether. "These ads don't work" and "There is no return on investment with PR" are common refrains of marketers who have limited clarity about who they are, a story to tell, or a product or service that gets people talking.

But when the foundational components of Formulaic marketing are indeed aligned and working together, collecting and organizing promotional tactics becomes more natural, more obvious, and more beneficial. Once your core elements are in place and aligned, there are a variety of simple tactics that you can use. While there are countless ideas of things you can do to promote the company, this chapter will address a number of basic areas to consider, many of which are interrelated and can function together.

Once some of the baseline components of Formulaic marketing are in place (elements like values, story, and audience awareness), promotional activities begin to seem more natural. Formulaic marketers implement promotional tactics that connect more precisely and deeply. Sporadic ads, sponsorships, and "stunts" become things of the past because of confidence in an identity and understanding of what a specific niche audience might respond to. And while paid advertising may very well be appropriate in certain cases, there are a number of less overt tactics that together comprise a well-orchestrated outreach effort: a balanced promotional attack that stems from the core.

Apply for an Award or Two

Growing up, I was taught to not brag about yourself, but to let your work do the talking instead. The wisdom of that, beyond simple humility, is that talking about your accomplishments doesn't carry as much weight with people as when others make their own remarks about what you achieve. If a restaurant owner tells me his food is excellent, I grow suspicious; if a mystery diner for a local publication tells me the same thing, I grow confident.

When it comes to your brand, applying for awards is one way to showcase your abilities and accomplishments through a third-party mouthpiece. Industry awards represent opportunities for your company to earn recognition through the objective and subjective criteria involved in the process.

There are awards of all types available for pursuit. Many industry associations have their own specific awards to recognize companies that accomplish something meaningful. The Association of Fundraising Professionals, for example, is a national organization that has local and national awards to honor fundraising innovation through an annual event called National Philanthropy Day. Beyond specific industry awards, there are also general business awards that are produced by local newspapers that honor things like "best places to work," "family-friendly workplaces," "fastest-growing companies," and so on.

Your company should make a habit of applying for some of these awards. They take time, employee participation, administrative follow-up, and even entry fees sometimes, but the benefits are tremendous. As our agency has navigated this circuit for the past several years, here are some of the positive outcomes I have noticed:

- Company pride—Team members feel better about where they work when the company earns recognition.
- Opportunities to improve—The objective criteria evaluated by the award committees show you where your company can get better, especially when you don't win.
- Goodwill—When you earn an award, people outside the organization notice and congratulate you.
- Enhanced credibility—Winning an award builds your credibility, especially since the awards are bestowed upon you by others.
- Visibility for the company—Awards are usually accompanied by announcements of some sort. Your company name and kudos are often featured in accompanying publications, on websites, and in other media. This exposure never hurts and costs nothing.

Some people think awards are a bit of a waste of time. I used to be one of them, especially since it takes time and resources to apply. Over the years, however, I've become a real believer. The benefits above are among the most prominent. If you keep your eyes open, awards that you might apply for are all around you.

Help Customers Find You When They're Not Looking

I went to the beach not too long ago and got all my stuff stolen. My backpack had my iPhone, my wallet, and my Kindle. What's worse, it had my car key, which proved to be really tough to deal with. I was stuck an hour from home with no way to start my car to get home. It was a mess.

Ever since then, I've been gun shy about going to the beach. As I've been thinking about going again, I have been considering ways to prevent this from happening again.

To make a plan, I typed "what are the best tools to hide your keys at the beach?" into Google and got a series of results. On page one of the results was a link to a page entitled "How to Keep Your Stuff Safe While Swimming," which led me to a page with a few helpful tips like "use the buddy system" and "leave your stuff in the hotel." But it also included a link to a product that the owner of the website sells, which it refers to as a portable safe, conceived to help people like me who need to secure valuables while traveling.

This type of Google query represents a moment in time when a customer most desperately needs your product. In my book *Found: Connecting with Customers in the Digital Age,* I refer to this as a "parachute moment." This is an example of how search engine optimization actually works. It's not about stuffing keywords into your web pages; it's about answering customer questions with quality content.

Your brand should be doing the same thing. Consider problems that your customer faces that your product could help with, and write about them like a journalist would. Notice in this example that the brand did *not* write about how great it was, how long it had been in business, and the like. It focused on the problem and kept the brand in the background.

Keep in mind that you can also use video to answer questions. Many people go right to YouTube when they want to solve some sort of problem in their life, repair something, or learn how to do something.

To get started, put yourself in the eyes of your customers and think like they do. If you own a cafe in Estes Park, Colorado, write posts with titles like "Interesting Places to Visit in Estes Park," "Cool

Restaurants in Estes Park," or "Best Times to Visit Estes Park." Too many brands want to focus on ranking high for "Cafes in Estes Park." The goal is to subtly introduce yourself to those searchers who might not even know they're looking for a cafe yet.

If you don't know where to begin in identifying topics to write about, here are some good questions to help you discover your customers' potential questions:

- What problems is our brand in a unique position to solve?
- When we interact with our customers, what questions do they typically ask us?
- What common threads do we see in our customers that might represent their needs or wants?
- What frustrations do our customers commonly have?
- What life events or experiences do our buyers have prior to finding us?

Anticipating your customers' questions and answering them with content is a great way to reach a customer who may not know they need you. Keep in mind that it takes time and patience. The blog post I mentioned above was written more than four years ago! The good news is that four years later, it's still drawing visitors.

Ask Your Customers to Get Social

The cool (and dangerous) thing about social media and user-generated media is that they happen on their own. Consumers have the technological and social power to create high-quality photos and videos and share them through global networks within an instant. And they do. Customers make up hashtags, memes, and the like without brands even saying a thing.

But they don't always think to do it. That's where brands can step in and play a role in guiding the social conversation (good, bad, or indifferent) and engagement with a brand. After all, research suggests that those customers who engage with brands online are likely to be more loyal, passionate, and talkative about the brand. I once got a shout-out from **vitamin**water and haven't ever forgotten it.

Publix Supermarkets gently nudges customers to share pictures of its sub sandwiches using their Instagram accounts with the #pubsub hashtag, which it prints on clings that stick to the deli case.

How hard is that? Not at all. I'm sure those stickers cost about zero dollars to produce. The payoff? For starters, participants are going to be giving Publix free promotion to their audiences—the equivalent of earned media. Perhaps more importantly, the users who participate are engaging with the brand in a way that builds the relationship between the customer and the product. Publix gets steady traction on Instagram and Facebook as a result. The benefits to Publix are so large, they're almost immeasurable.

Admittedly, not all of us have the foot traffic, volume, and photogenic product offering that Publix does with its subs, but we can learn something substantial from its success: remind your customers to talk about you online. If you're delivering a positive experience to them, you'll be glad you did.

Teach Your Customers Something

What do you remember about your favorite teacher growing up? Mine was smart, encouraging, supportive, resourceful, and helpful. Those who teach—and teach well—occupy a special place in our hearts and minds. They are leaders, guides, and advocates. And we trust them.

Brands have the same opportunity. As marketers, we have the opportunity to build relationships and trust through education. Every product or service is made better through what we know about it—and what we can share with others. That product's maker is best positioned to do just that. And you have the opportunity to take the lead.

Here are a few examples of how a brand can teach:

- The maker of a particular medication can explain to you when to take it, what to expect, and how to proceed if you have a problem.
- A theme park can teach you how to get there, what to bring, and how to make the most of your experience.
- A law firm can instruct you regarding what to expect during your consultation, what to bring, and what it's like to go to court.

Your best outlets for teaching are your blog, social media, and your marketing materials. (In addition to your in-person interactions, of course.) One company, River Pools & Spas, was recently profiled in the *New York Times* for its successful approach to growing sales through teaching. The company did this by listening to customer questions, "making everyone a teacher," and answering them online.[40]

As you think about ways to attract and grow customer relationships, teach. You'll help your customers and your business.

Do Something Visible

Instead of just telling your audience members what you do and how you are different, show them. You know the cliché about "actions speaking louder than words." Well, it's true. Instead of *saying* something to capture attention, try *doing* something (visible) to demonstrate your message, values, or focus.

There are many ways to find something visible to do within the context of your brand. Consider Nathan Clark of Wondermade, the craft marshmallow maker, who decided to go on an ice-cream only diet to launch his specialty ice creams. Friends and fans followed him through his journey on Kickstarter and Facebook with his new product at the center. Instead of just talking about ice cream, he ate it continually to the delight of his fans.

Or consider Foundry Commercial who was looking for a way to stand out in the commercial real estate sector and to demonstrate some of its core elements. To celebrate its corporate value of service, the company held its first-ever annual ServeWeek by sending employees out to volunteer in area non-profit organizations. Paul Ellis, Foundry CEO, visited the company's offices throughout the week to show support across the entire enterprise. The week was a big hit in the community and a positive catalyst within the culture.

Sometimes, doing something is more powerful than saying something. Look for ways to demonstrate what you do in a tangible, visible way.

Earn Media Coverage by Pitching Your Blogs to Journalists

Once you commit to a teaching your customers and sharing your stories, a blog is a great outlet for publishing. Creating stories around your company and its people, customers, and products can be a great way to make your site interesting, engage an audience, populate your social feed, and earn some search engine traffic along the way.

There are many great corporate blogs out there that you might explore to gain some inspiration. Watchmaker Shinola of Detroit, Michigan, has a great corporate blog (https://www.shinola.com/thejournal/), where the company shares stories about its products, artisans, beliefs, and values. Publix Supermarkets is another company that has a great blog (https://blog.publix.com/publix/), where stories and content engages, inspires, and connects with shoppers.

But one little-known promotional tactic that works quite well is taking the stories published by your content team and pitching them to journalists who need content for publications. Our agency has had success in landing placements in prominent publications like *Fortune, Forbes*, and *Business Insider,* just by sharing what we have written when we see journalists querying the media landscape for sources and/or content.

Contently recently published a feature story on this phenomenon that shows how General Mills, maker of cereals like Cheerios, Wheaties, and others, has landed major media placements using its company blog, *Taste* (http://www.blog.generalmills.com/). *Taste* features pieces on products, sustainability, and innovation as well as human interest stories. The General Mills team publishes stories "the media wasn't picking up on" and earns media placement along the way. "In many instances, *Taste* gives journalists a reason to pick up the phone and call us," explains Kevin Hunt of General Mills. They've landed media placements in outlets like the *New York Times* by following this formula.

If you're already blogging on behalf of your brand, keep going! If you are producing content suitable for media outlets on a regular basis, take the next step and begin sharing your ideas and stories with journalists. You might find yourself quickly on the way to major media placements that you never thought possible.

Ask Your Customers What They Really Think

How happy are your customers with you? It's a tough question to answer because customers are not always easy to please. Customers are our lifeblood, but we don't always know how happy they are with us. Over time, I've noticed that many companies would rather not ask, fearing that they'd be inviting criticism, opening a can of worms, poking the bear, and so on. In short, they play the "ignorance is bliss" card.

The problem with this approach, though, is that most people won't tell you when they're dissatisfied, you won't know there's a problem, and you won't be able to fix it. According to a survey by service expert Ruby Newell-Legner, only 4 percent of dissatisfied customers will actually complain. The other 96 percent will simply vote with their feet by never returning or, even worse, telling their friends that your business failed them. In short, a lack of complaints doesn't indicate customer satisfaction. If you want to know how customers feel, you have to ask. Don't assume the best.

I know what you're thinking:

- I hate customer surveys.
- None of my customers will fill out a long survey.
- We're different, and our customers would tell us.

I would respectfully disagree. The good news is that the survey doesn't have to be long. In fact, according to consultant Fred Reichheld of Bain & Company, all you need to do is ask one question. In his book *The Ultimate Question*, Reichheld argues that you only need to ask one question of your customers: "On a scale of 0 to 10, how likely is it that you would recommend this company to a friend or colleague?"

The author's research, explained in his book, tells us that the average score to this question tells us if our business is growing or not. If the experience we deliver is so good that our customers would recommend us to a friend, we're good to go.

Another hidden element of this process is that we can actually improve customer loyalty simply by asking how satisfied customers are. According to research in the *Harvard Business Review*, customers who are asked about their satisfaction are more loyal, more profitable, and likely to spend more than those who aren't surveyed. Why? The authors suggest that consumers like to be "coddled," which asking them does. It also reinforces positive feelings by demonstrating concern. Asking how satisfied I am shows me you care.[41]

> Customers who are asked about their satisfaction are more loyal, more profitable, and likely to spend more than those who aren't.
>
> Harvard Business Review

Ruby Red Cleaning, the company that cleans my home, finds out how satisfied its customers are with its maid services by asking a simple question via e-mail.

When I get the survey, I feel like the company has its act together and that it cares. In my mind, the effort demonstrates that customer satisfaction is on the company's radar screen.

Automating these types of surveys is pretty simple now, with all the online tools available to do so. If you're not asking your customers how happy they are, I encourage you to begin. And even if they don't tell you how they feel, just asking may help you get closer to them anyway.

Formulaic marketers know how to use these and other, subtler promotional attacks to meet the needs of customer segments. While paid advertising is always an option, creating your own content, engaging your audience in social media, and even asking customers about their satisfaction level can go a long way. And once your baseline Formulaic marketing components are in place, inventive promotional opportunities will jump right out to you.

CHAPTER 10

PATIENCE AND DISCIPLINE

> The last step [of marketing] is so often overlooked: The part where you show up, regularly, consistently and generously, for years and years, to organize and lead and build confidence in the change you seek to make.
>
> —Seth Godin

I've read somewhere that while it only takes an evening for a mushroom to sprout up, it can take one hundred years for an oak tree to grow. The former is short lived, simple, and temporary, while the latter is enduring, complex, and a long-term creation to behold. Important developments in commerce and brands happen over sustained periods of time—not overnight or by the end of next week.

Similarly, the marketing process takes time. Cultivating customer relationships takes time. This requires patience, and it requires discipline. If those two elements are not in place, your marketing will fail or, more accurately, you'll quit before your success has the time to materialize.

As an illustration, let me explain how this plays out in our agency. Recently, I paused and reflected on some new clients who had signed on with our agency and the process by which they went from being aware of us to being actual buyers of our services. These client "wins" had come to fruition through a variety of means. When I stop to look back and think about how they came to the point at which they signed agreements with us, each client took a slightly different path. Here are a couple of examples:

- A device manufacturer who first learned of our firm more than five years ago, through a friend of a friend struck up a relationship, had lunch a few times, and ultimately hired us to build a website.
- A commercial developer was referred to us through a colleague of the firm who had never worked with us directly but got to know the firm through some joint volunteer work we had done with a chamber of commerce over nearly a decade.
- A professional services firm engaged us in an interesting piece of work after getting to know our team through joint service in a civic organization.
- A construction firm signed on with us after reading a piece of material we had written and distributing it to his colleagues. We first connected on Facebook.

I wish I was smart enough to be able to go back in time and know how all these activities that we undertook months and years ago were going to add up to sales months or years later, but I'm not. There's no crystal ball—not then and not now. All I can tell you for sure is that all these prospects took different paths and lengths of time to become our customers, being gently affected by our marketing efforts along the way. Steve Jobs said it best when he explained in his now-famous commencement address that "you can't connect the dots looking forward; you can only connect them looking backward."

I can tell you, however, that there were several common threads in these transactions:

- They became aware of our firm in some way.
- They used our website to perform initial research on our firm and compare us to other agencies.
- They visited our office to meet us and see our facility.
- They received marketing collateral from us and distributed it internally.
- They were given (and presumably read) thought-leadership material that we had published in print and online.
- They took their time before writing us a check.

Our business and your business are being evaluated all the time by the marketplace. Each customer takes his or her own course to get to the point at which the check is signed, but customers encounter your marketing materials (investments you have made) all along the way. As they move from stranger to check writer, they are exposed to

- your website,
- your blog posts,
- your social media updates,
- your business card,
- your printed collateral, and
- your logo.

Having all these things in order is the right thing to do. You can't isolate any one of these activities and determine the individual dividends it pays. It's just like you can't measure the potential value of an event you choose to attend or a sales inquiry you make with a prospect.

Does all this mean that you should not measure the performance of your marketing activities? Of course not. It just means that you should look at the intangibles that won't show up in the metrics on your spreadsheet. Formulaic marketing takes time, patience, and discipline.

The Danger of ROI

Do you measure the marketing return on investment (ROI) of having a presentable office lobby? Do you count how many leads you captured from spending an hour of your time with a community connector who invited you to have a cup of coffee? Of course you don't. You can't.

So why do marketers insist on demanding an immediate return on a blog post or Facebook spend? Or on a Google Adwords campaign? Or use a lack of same-day purchase metrics as an excuse to abandon social media efforts?

I will never be able to calculate the ROI of the marketing materials we produce. Or tell you what would have happened if we never invested in a content marketing strategy that includes blog posts, books, and white papers. I can just tell you that it works and you should do it.

The reason this is so important is that too many marketers are searching for measurable returns on digital marketing activities that they will never be able to demonstrate. In some cases, they end up not doing the right thing because the short-term return can't be immediately seen.

Whether it's off-line or online, where you choose to spend your marketing dollars should be a matter of art as well as science. Measure, certainly, but don't let measurement keep you from doing the right thing. I would encourage you to follow Jobs's follow-on advice: trust that the dots will somehow connect in the future.

Marketing Isn't a Jukebox

The most difficult question a client asks an agency person is this: How much return on my investment can I expect? In other words, how many widgets will I sell or appointments will I book if I proceed with this public relations effort/social media campaign/re-brand/event sponsorship/you get the idea?

My answer: I dunno.

You see, marketing just isn't a jukebox. You don't put in a quarter and immediately see (or hear) the result. It just doesn't work that way.

Sure, there are metrics to follow and ways to track campaigns and beans to count, but marketing isn't always linear. Consumer behavior isn't always confined to a pretty spreadsheet. Why? Because consumers buy in different ways at different times and for different reasons. It doesn't mean that you shouldn't count things—you should. But numbers don't always tell the whole story...or, as Albert Einstein said, "not everything that counts can be counted."

Consumers interact with brands through Google searches, word-of-mouth interaction, first-hand experiences, social media exposure, and countless other ways. It might take a consumer seven or eight interactions over the course of six to twelve months to pull the trigger on an inquiry or a purchase. And you can't always identify the catalyst(s).

> Not everything that can be counted counts.
>
> —— Albert Einstein

The more informed question for the marketer is this: What is the cost of not doing the right thing? What is the cost of not creating blog posts to respond to those Google searches? What is the cost of not being present on social media to guide the customer along that nine-month path to purchase? What is the cost of not being visible in the media through public relations efforts? I'll tell you what it is: it's invisibility and irrelevance.

I'll say it another way. I visited my doctor recently, and he asked me "Matt, have you had your flu shot yet?" When I told him I hadn't and didn't want one, he shook his head and said "OK, well, call me when you get the flu, I guess." He was right. He can't guarantee me that I won't get the flu, but doing the right thing is always the right thing to do, even if you can't measure it.

It's right to be focused on metrics. But marketing involves risk. Just because you can't guarantee the results of your marketing doesn't mean you should refrain from it altogether. That's just operating from a place of fear.

How Growth Really Happens

Every marketer wants his or her business to grow and thrive. That's what marketing is about. But let's really think about what growth actually is, how it happens, what it looks like, and how you know it's happening.

To do this, let's look at botanical growth—how plant life grows, develops, and thrives. Harkening back to our comparison of the overnight mushroom and the one-hundred-year oak tree, we can learn a lot by thinking about how plants and trees grow.

I wasn't really good at the hard sciences when I was a kid. I came to take my professors' word for it that electricity and gravity were real things that operated under established laws. I'm not sure I can explain botanical growth, either, but I can tell you about some simple truths we can observe and count on with respect to how it works. Just like I know that sticking a metal fork into an electrical outlet will shock you, I can tell you similar things about how plants grow.

For starters, growth begins with a seed of some sort. It happens when a tree sheds a seed or when I buy a package of seeds from Home Depot. It all begins with a seed. In marketing and promotion, those seeds are things like ideas, press releases, blog posts, introductions to decision makers, Facebook ads, and whatever else we can dream up.

Nothing happens until that seed is planted. If I never open that package of seeds from Home Depot and put one in the ground, nothing begins. In terms of marketing, no growth can happen without showing that press release to a journalist or turning on that Facebook promotion with your credit card.[42]

Once the seed is planted in good soil and watered a bit, things start happening underneath the ground. Germination begins. That seed starts developing a bit underground by forming roots and sprouting toward the sky. To the planter, though, it looks like nothing is happening. Same for the marketer. It may appear for some time that growth is not occurring because it's not visible. But just because you can't see it doesn't mean it's not happening.

As the seed sprouts out of the ground into a sapling and starts reaching for the sky, it needs more things to keep evolving. It has always needed water and nutrients from the soil. It takes in the sunlight and the carbon dioxide as it propels upward and outward. All the while, the growth happens slowly—gradually. It happens so slowly, in fact, that we can never really see it occurring. It's too slow and gradual for us to observe. But that doesn't mean it's not taking place.

Ultimately, that seed turns into something much bigger and more fully developed—a plant, a shrub, or a tree. It bears fruit, ultimately, but that takes a sustained period of growth—a full cycle or handful of months or years for anything to come from it. The harvest (or customer acquisition) never happens in the same season as the planting of the seed. It always comes later.

What's also important to note is that what ultimately springs out of the ground can be different from what we expected. You never know what you might get. I've seen gardens have a row of towering plants containing an unexpected runt or two. I've witnessed strange sprouts and off-shoot branches surprise and delight. I've also seen gargantuan plants emerge that tower over their nearby peers. Growth is simply unpredictable.

The grower's patience, though, yields something much bigger than the fruit. The fully formed plant produces more seeds, which can be replanted right along that one for the next period of growth. All from that single, original seed that came out of the package. The process goes on and on through the grower's discipline, time, and patience.

I am sure that you see the parallel here. Growth in business shares many facets with botanical growth. Fruit takes time to emerge, but it only does so once seeds are planted, care is taken to grow them, and the grower waits. Strong organisms require patience and discipline.

Customer Relationships Take Time

Our deepest, strongest friendships in life are forged over years and decades—not days and weeks. We usually don't run to people we met yesterday when we're having a crisis today.

Relationships with brands are the same way. We build trust with our customers over an extended period of time—not with a single pay-per-click ad or Facebook post. Yet sustained relationships in which people actually hand over their hard-earned dollars don't occur in an instant. There are exceptions, of course. We're all occasionally prone to an impulse purchase or two, but that's not the norm.

Using our example of botanical growth and how a seed grows into a tree over time, would it be sensible to plant a seed one day and then get frustrated two days later when you checked on it and saw nothing? Of course not. You would need to water it daily for several days or weeks, perhaps along with a little fertilizer and some good weather, before you saw the first sign of progress, let alone something substantial.

The same thinking goes for customer relationships. They take time and multiple iterations and touch points to germinate. There's no hard and fast rule for how many times you must communicate with a potential customer before, but we can safely assume that it's usually more than one or two. Marketing expert Dr. Jeffrey Lant, in fact, teaches us that we should plan on seven. Lant's "Rule of Seven" states that "to penetrate the buyer's consciousness and make significant penetration in a given market, you have to [communicate with] the prospect a minimum of seven times within an eighteen-month period." So give yourself some time, be patient, and plan on more than one or two instance of communication with a prospect before he or she buys something.

Customers Aren't Zombies

If you asked most marketers, the goal of digital marketing is conversion. For the sake of this illustration, let's define a *conversion* as a purchase of an online product. The word *conversion* is used because the goal is to convert a web visitor to a buyer. The more conversions, the more revenue. The more revenue, the more profits.

Since not every visitor will buy (in fact, most visitors don't buy anything at all), marketers typically study the ratio between buyers and visitors. If you sell your product to three out of every one hundred visitors, your conversion rate is 3 percent. Naturally, the aim of efficient promotion is to increase that conversion rate, so you sell to as many visitors as possible.

As a marketer who is striving to increase efficiency, you might measure the profitability of your promotional activity by analyzing the cost of attracting those one hundred visitors and analyzing the overall viability of the investment. If it costs $1,000 to attract those one hundred visitors, the cost-per-conversion comes in at $333.33. The marketer then has to evaluate this rate and decide whether the spend is worthwhile: that figure is a total failure if you are selling a $29 widget, but a complete success if you are selling a $5,000 cruise to Alaska.

The scenario above is not particularly challenging to grasp, and it's certainly not new. In fact, this concept of conversion is taught at seminar after seminar and relayed in blogs, tweets, and books on this subject. And while most marketers would agree on the methodology, it's inherently flawed.

The scenario above is based on the notion that buyers of products are zombies with credit cards. In other words, it paints a picture of one hundred passive, ignorant consumers going through a line in lock-step, while only three of them whip out an American Express card and buy the product. It also assumes that the ratio calculation will hold for the next one hundred zombies to come through the line. While I wish the scenario was this simple, it's not. Not by a long shot. The truth is, those who carry credit cards aren't zombies.

Today's consumers (the people who actually do have credit cards) have more options, knowledge, control, discernment, and discretion than ever before. They are bombarded with more messages in a day than they can possibly hope to process. (Some estimates say between three thousand and twenty thousand.) They look to friends for recommendations, make purchase decisions on their own time, and are reflective and thoughtful about financial decisions. The assumption that a cleverly crafted social media or Google ad campaign is going to consistently coax consumers to plunk down their credit cards to fit within the confines of a marketer's metrics spreadsheet is inherently flawed. Things simply don't work this way.

The idea of data gathering, measuring performance, and optimizing marketing results are all good, constructive activities to embrace. But assuming that the underlying results will emanate from a "set it and forget it" approach to promotion and results is asking for disappointment.

So how does the marketer move from the idea of a hands-off marketing funnel to a more practical and realistic approach? While I'm not sure that there is a simple answer, there are some truths that marketers would do well to ponder and embrace. Here are some of those truths that, when applied to a specific marketing challenge, would lead toward a more satisfying digital-marketing approach:

- **Conversions are rarely instantaneous**—It usually takes multiple interactions with a brand before we ultimately pull the trigger. The old marketing adage called the Rule of Seven tells us that it takes seven interactions with a brand before most of us buy. In today's hyperconnected, always-on world, that number is probably closer to seventy-seven than seven.

- **Facebook likes are worth something**—It's hard to say for sure exactly how much, but a consumer's choice to connect with you on Facebook, Twitter, or another social media site is an opportunity for you to build a relationship. So don't minimize or waste it.

- **Your social media content must be worthy**—People rarely subscribe to your social media content to be nice. They do it to gain something: an idea, a tip, entertainment, a deal, or just to remember you. Before they make that decision, they'll look to see how valuable your messaging is. So make it count. Be informative, helpful, and/or funny—be of benefit. And keep doing it, so that they stay subscribed.

- **Your product must be remarkable**—This is tough for most marketers when they see disappointing sales figures. But it is important to remember that the first *P* in the four *P*s of marketing is product. Your product must be valuable, even indispensable. If it's not, the rest of the four *P*s (price, place, promotion) won't do you a ton of good. (Hint: Part of social media really succeeding for you is having people speak well of you on social media because of how highly they think of your product. So make the product so remarkable that people can't help but tell their friends.)

- **Consumers are skeptical**—People don't often buy from people they don't know or trust. Brands must build that trust. And that doesn't occur in a Google Adword or a broadcast e-mail message. It happens over time through their interactions with you, the recommendations of their friends, product reviews posted by strangers, and the content you create.

- **Marketers must have patience**—People don't all buy immediately. They think about it first. Consumers like to flip through pages, kick tires, ask their friends, and go for test drives. So have patience. If your initial clicks don't turn into dollars within the first nanosecond, it doesn't mean that your promotions have failed. It means that they've just begun. Expecting otherwise may set you up for disappointment.

- **Google rewards content**—We all look for things on Google. That's how we behave. Your product's buyers are looking for you right now but don't know it yet. Google will introduce them to you if you provide thoughtful, relevant content on a consistent basis. That's the essence of how Google works— it rewards the authentic marketer who writes and produces content. So write—well and often.

- **Some diseases don't have cures**—So while hoping for a miracle is encouraged, expecting one is probably not wise. In marketing, there are very few miracles—defined as a bunch of buyers logging on and giving you a credit card at a hefty profit. Plan, instead, on a slower, more gradual process in which sales are earned over time—not in an instant. If you're looking for quick and easy—well, that's akin to asking a physician for a cure that doesn't exist. You can beat up the doctor all you want, but it won't change the facts.

There are many more truths that we could discuss here, but the essence remains: today's consumers are smarter, savvier, and more discerning than ever. They're the ones with the credit cards. So if your conversions don't come through a predictable, well-formed funnel, you're probably doing something right—creating authentic, long-lasting customer relationships.

All of these illustrations and metaphors might be perceived as reasons not to measure things or to hold marketers and agency folks like me accountable for the actions that they take and the investments that they make. Not so. It's just a call to consider that marketing and growth take time and that not all the things that we can measure and count are significant. The financier who saved Nike from certain collapse in 1975 described this line of thinking as "stupidity" and quipped that "people pay too much attention to numbers." Albert Einstein said it another way: "not everything that can be counted counts." As a marketer, trust the numbers and performance, but don't forget or dismiss the development of the seeds that might be happening underneath the soil, invisible to the naked eye. And Formulaic marketers are willing to wait.

EPILOGUE

Thriving companies don't flourish simply because their branding is cool, their ads are clever, or because they have a killer website. While none of these surface elements hurt, they can't replace a Formulaic marketing approach stems from the core—the inside.

A brand that is at the top of its game is likely doing a number of things well in concert, in perpetuity, and with purpose.

It has taken the time to understand and articulate who it is, what it stands for, and why it does what it does. It's written on the wall somewhere and lived out by each member of the team.

The team is galvanized by a well-documented culture that represents a common framework for how things will be done within the company in ways that are consistent and distinguishable. The company hires, fires, and trains using this blueprint.

The brand has stories to tell about its origination and customers. The company collects these stories and tells them frequently in order to amplify and perpetuate its message.

It also can point to clear differences in the company that separate it from competitors very distinctively. These differences are often courageous in nature because they might alienate some would-be buyers.

That's not necessarily a bad thing, though, because *not* being attractive to everyone is the point. The thriving brand serves narrow and specific audience segments with the understanding that it can't serve everyone.

And because it knows the audience so intimately, what it delivers as a product—the total customer experience—fits hand in glove with the expectations of the buyer.

Promotion naturally becomes easier because it understands what to say, to whom it should communicate, and in what channel the message should travel. And since the product and audience fit so well together, the word-of-mouth effect naturally happens and supports the promotional effort.

Thriving brands grow over time. It takes decades, not weeks, to thrive and flourish fully. And because they understand this, a thriving brand is patient.

COLOPHON

Songs that kept the author company during writing and editing:
- "There Will Be Time"—Mumford & Sons
- "Denial"—Hoyle
- "The World Is Ours"—Volunteer
- "Birds"—Coldplay
- "Casual Party"—Band of Horses
- "One Step at a Time"—Luke Reynolds
- "One Dance"—Drake, Whizkid, Kyla
- "Good Help (Is So Hard to Find)"—Death Cab for Cutie
- "Wow"—Beck
- "Burn the Witch"—Radiohead
- "Electric"—Brett
- "It Comes Back to You"—Imagine Dragons
- "CLEAR"—NEEDTOBREATHE
- "Kings and Queens"—Brooke Fraser
- "Psalm 51"—Life.Church Worship
- "Prince of Peace"—Hillsong United
- "WALLS"—Kings of Leon
- "Future Looks Good"—OneRepublic

Equipment used to organize and produce the manuscript:
- Apple MacBook Pro
- Apple Magic Mouse 2
- iPad
- iPhone

- Evernote
- Microsoft Word
- Google Docs
- Scrivener

MARKETING TIP MONDAY

Marketing Tip Monday

{ One free marketing idea in your inbox every Monday }

| Email Address | SUBSCRIBE |

Marketing Tip Monday is a weekly email publication that you can expect to receive every...Monday. Issues are composed, compiled, and curated by Matt Certo, a marketing practitioner who has run a digital agency for over 20 years and author of Found: Connecting with Customers in the Digital Age. You can expect interesting ideas that are working, practical things you can try, and best practices from the front lines. Give it a shot for a couple weeks and unsubscribe if you hate it.

Marketing is an ongoing journey that never stops. For more ideas and insights, sign up for a free weekly marketing tip from the author at www.MarketingTipMonday.com.

ENDNOTES

1   Coca-Cola corporate web site, https://www.worldofcoca-cola.com/explore/explore-inside/explore-vault-secret-formula/

2   Wikipedia entry, Google PageRank https://en.wikipedia.org/wiki/PageRank

3   Wikipedia entry, The Soup Nazi, https://en.wikipedia.org/wiki/The_Soup_Nazi

4   Southwest Airlines corporate web site, https://www.southwest.com/html/about-southwest/careers/culture.html

5   TED corporate web site, https://www.ted.com/talks/simon_sinek_how_great_leaders_inspire_action

6   *Shoe Dog: A Memoir by the Creator of Nike*, Phil Knight, Scribner, 2016, p. 273

7   Nemours corporate web site, https://www.nemours.org/about/mission.html

8   Drew Houston of Dropbox: Figure Out the Things You Don't Know, *The New York Times, Adam Bryant*, June 3, 2016

9   Microsoft corporate web site, https://www.microsoft.com/en-us/about/

10 Ritz-Carlton corporate web site, http://www.ritzcarlton.com/en/about/gold-standards

11 Management by Fire: A Conversation with Chef Anthony Bourdain, *Harvard Business Review*, July 2002, Gardiner Morse

12 http://www.businessinsider.com/inside-facebooks-little-red-book-2015-5

13 Zappos corporate web site, https://www.zapposinsights.com/culture-book

14 *Let My People Go Surfing*, Yvon Chouinard, Penguin Books, 2016, p. 69

15 How Google Attracts the World's Best Talent, http://fortune.com/2014/09/04/how-google-attracts-the-worlds-best-talent/

16 Want to Work in 18 Miles of Books? First, the Quiz, Annie Correal, *The New York Times*, July 15, 2016

17 Slideshare entry, http://www.slideshare.net/whatidiscover/crispin-porter-bogusky-employee-handbook

18 Stanford University web site, http://news.stanford.edu/2005/06/14/jobs-061505/

19 *Let My People Go Surfing*, Yvon Chouinard, Penguin Books, 2016, p. 137

20 Why Your Brain Loves Good Storytelling, *Harvard Business Review*, Paul J. Zak, https://hbr.org/2014/10/why-your-brain-loves-good-storytelling

21 Why Sharing Stories Brings People Together, *Psychology Today*, June 6, 2011, Joshua Gowin, Ph.D.

22 *The Social Cognitive Neuroscience of Leading Organizational Change*, Robert A. Snyder

23 With Chobani Back on Track, Founder is Staying Put, Craig Giammona, *Bloomberg Businessweek*, September 10, 2015

24 Sales Are Exploding for the Little-known Soda Brand with a Cult Following, Hayley Peterson, October 8, 2016, *Business Insider* http://www.businessinsider.com/lacroix-sales-are-exploding-2015-10

25 Whole Foods corporate web site, http://www.wholefoodsmarket.com/about-our-products/quality-standards/food-ingredient

26 *Contagious: Why Things Catch On*, Jonah Berger, Simon & Schuster p. 42

27 Branding in the Digital Age: You're Spending Your Money in All the Wrong Places, *Harvard Business Review*, December 2010, David C. Edelman

[28] How Two Brothers Turned a $300 Cooler into a $450 Million Cult Brand, *Inc. Magazine*, Bill Saporito, http://www.inc.com/magazine/201602/bill-saporito/yeti-coolers-founders-roy-ryan-seiders.html

[29] Lululemon Calls its Ideal Customers 'Ocean' and 'Duke' – Here's Everything We Know About Them, *Business Insider*, February 2, 2015, Ashley Lutz

[30] Wikipedia entry, Marketing Mix, https://en.wikipedia.org/wiki/Marketing_mix

[31] Bobbi Brown corporate web site, https://www.bobbibrowncosmetics.com/about-bobbi

[32] Marshmallows, Chasing Wisdom Podcast, http://www.northlandchurch.net/podcast/nathan_clark/

[33] YouTube Video, https://www.youtube.com/watch?v=NI9w-vvDR9o The Story of Scotty Cameron

[34] Publishers Take on Ad-Agency Roles with Branded Content, *The Wall Street Journal*, December 11, 2016

[35] *Found: Connecting With Customers in the Digital Age*, Matthew W. Certo, p. 18, Findsome & Winmore Press.

[36] Google corporate web site, https://support.google.com/webmasters/answer/6001093?hl=en

[37] How the General Mills Newsroom Became an Earned Media Machine, *The Content Strategist*, Arik Hanson, October 16, 2015

[38] John Mellencamp corporate web site, http://www.mellencamp.com/news.html?n_id=914

[39] *Youtility: Why Smart Marketing is about Help Not Hype*, Jay Bear, Penguin, 2014

[40] A Revolutionary Marketing Strategy: Answer Customers' Questions, *The New York Times, Mark Cohen*, February 27, 2013

[41] How Surveys Influence Customers, *Harvard Business Review*, Paul M. Dholakia and Vicki G. Morwitz, May 2002.

[42] Laws of Sowing and Reaping, Rick Warren, https://www.youtube.com/watch?v=zLXyj3n3pJ0

61199285R00085

Made in the USA
Middletown, DE
08 January 2018